Climate Law - Current Opportunities and Challenges

CLIMATE LAW - CURRENT OPPORTUNITIES AND CHALLENGES

ESSAYS FROM THE OFFICIAL OPENING OF CLIMLAW: GRAZ

EVA SCHULEV - STEINDL, OLIVER C. RUPPEL AND
FERDINAND KERSCHNER (EDS.)

eleven

Published, sold and distributed by Eleven
P.O. Box 85576
2508 CG The Hague
The Netherlands
Tel.: +31 70 33 070 33
Fax: +31 70 33 070 30
email: sales@elevenpub.nl
www.elevenpub.com

Sold and distributed in USA and Canada
Independent Publishers Group
814 N. Franklin Street
Chicago, IL 60610, USA
Order Placement: +1 800 888 4741
Fax: +1 312 337 5985
orders@ipgbook.com
www.ipgbook.com

Eleven is an imprint of Boom uitgevers Den Haag.

Research Center ClimLaw: Graz, University of Graz, Universitätsplatz 3, 8010 Graz, Austria https://climlaw.uni-graz.at/en/.

ISBN 978-94-6236-237-6

Acknowledgments

We express our gratitude for the printing subsidy provided by the Climate Change Centre Austria in cooperation with the Climate and Energy Fund.

This Open Access publication was realised with funding from the University of Graz.

Foreword

On 17 June 2020, we 'celebrated' the official opening of the new Research Center for Climate Law at the University of Graz (ClimLaw: Graz) in the midst of the COVID-19 pandemic. More than one year later, it is with great pleasure and satisfaction that we assemble the essays from the presentations delivered at the official opening of ClimLaw: Graz.

The presentations comprised interventions from distinguished members of the Scientific Advisory Board of ClimLaw: Graz and shorter presentations from various PhD students. These shorter contributions are based on blog posts that have already been published as part of the blog "Junge Wissenschaft im Öffentlichen Recht" (juwiss.de) in German. This publication is therefore not meant as a purely scientific effort but, in the first place, as a testimony of what has been presented at the official launch of ClimLaw: Graz.

With the various essays, we want to highlight some current opportunities and challenges pertaining to climate law. These essays have, for the purpose of this publication, been assembled in either Part I or Part II thereof.

In Part I, the range of essays deals with 'Avoiding Climate Catastrophe: Mission Impossible or Realistic Ambition? The Challenges and Potential Crowbars to Stem the Tide'; 'Climate Law and Climate Science: Joint Enabler for a New Climate Enlightenment?'; and 'Against the Taming of the Spinners – On the National Goal of Climate Protection'. These essays complement each other splendidly as they sketch some pertinent questions of climate law from different interdisciplinary, geographical and timely angles.

In Part II, we are delighted to present selected contemporary aspects of national and international climate law from different substantive perspectives. Earlier in 2021, United States Special Envoy for Climate, John Kerry, stated that it is now that we have "the last best chance" to save our planet and avoid a climate catastrophe.

Winston Churchill once said, "success is not final, failure is not fatal: it is the courage to continue that counts". In this light, one essay is suitably titled 'It is not the winning but the taking part that counts: the symbolic and indirect effects of strategic climate litigation'. The further range of Part II contributions is substantively wide, dealing with 'Legitimate Expectations', State Subsidies and Climate Change Mitigation; 'WTO Rules on Border Carbon Adjustment for the EU ETS: Key GATT Principles'; 'Balancing Decisions in Climate Law: How economic instruments could help to increase their acceptance'; 'Resettlements as Spatial Adaptation Measures to Tackle Climate Change Impacts?'; 'The European Green Deal – What's in a Name?' and 'The Ecuadorian Chevron Judgement: Blueprint for a Neo-constitutional Environmental Law?'.

All the essays in this publication – in one way or another – reflect that climate change is an indiscriminating challenge unlike anything humanity has encountered before. Therefore, climate law is an essential emerging discipline to urgently stabilise the concentration of greenhouse gases in the atmosphere, especially CO_2, at a certain level to prevent dangerous anthropogenic interference with the climate system, embedded in a multi-level system of international, European and national regulations, which are closely and inherently interlinked with many other areas of law.

COVID-19 provided all of us with an unprecedented opportunity to reflect upon and to fully consider the implications of preparation when confronted with a disaster of global proportion. The response to COVID-19 serves as an example of how we can either respond or continue to ignore alarming climate change warnings. It is our sincere hope that solutions to COVID-19 can now be aligned to those of the climate crisis for a global transformation towards more sustainability, resilience, equity, and justice. Both crises necessitate that environmental protection and sustainability are centre stage in political thinking, action and diplomacy. In this effort, the law has an indispensable role to play in the mitigation and adaptation to climate change, which require effective regulation, strategies and roadmaps, affecting all spheres of human activities, including behaviour and lifestyle change, individuals and communities, in all regions and nations, across all sectors and across the world.

In light of the aforementioned, we are optimistic that our research center ClimLaw: Graz will contribute to this mammoth task and continue to shed further light on legal aspects related to one of the greatest challenges of our time. Ultimately, the research center's task is to critically observe and analyse current developments in climate law from an Austrian, European and global perspective, and to carry out research projects with a focus on climate law in its widest sense, bringing together national and international partners from the legal fraternity, climate science and practice. Due to its close links with climate science, climate economics, climate ethics, etc., and its intensive cooperation with stakeholders, ClimLaw: Graz is designed to be truly transdisciplinary and as such aims to become a globally recognised competent partner for exchange, scientific reports, expert information and legal advice. The diverse range of courses offered by the center's members introduces law students at under- and postgraduate levels, as well as students of other fields of study, to climate law in its multiple facets. In doing so, ClimLaw: Graz is envisaged to become a nationally and internationally connected research and teaching platform. The center organises and designs scientific conferences, workshops in cooperation with a wide range of partners from academia, science, policy and practice. We are proud that our research center for climate law at the Faculty of Law of the University of Graz is also part of different global distinguished University networks and the interdisciplinary Field of Excellence 'Climate Change Graz' of the University of Graz, an association of researchers who jointly research and share their knowledge on climate change and sustainability.

We would like to cordially thank all the contributors to this publication, Eleven for their professional services as well as Julia Wallner for her valuable assistance in making this book formally publishable.

Last but by no way least, we need to thank the University of Graz Rector, Professor Martin Polaschek and the Dean of the University of Graz Faculty of Law, Professor Christoph Bezemek for their continued support in the further development of ClimLaw: Graz.

Professor Eva Schulev-Steindl, Founding Director ClimLaw
Professor Oliver C. Ruppel, Co-Director ClimLaw

Graz and Stellenbosch, August 2021

TABLE OF CONTENTS

Avoiding Climate Catastrophe: Mission Impossible or Realistic Ambition?

The Challenges and Potential Crowbars to Stem the Tide

Jaap Spier[*]

> *Si l'on veut un effet boule de neige, il faut lancer la première boule, sans attendre que le changement climatique fasse disparaître la neige.*[1]

1 Introduction

At the time of writing, the subject of COVID-19 claims the attention of both politicians and others. The debate about COVID-19 and climate change is marked by common rhetoric about the urgency of the need to take action.

In September 2020, "political leaders participating in the United Nations Summit on biodiversity" rightly noted that "we are in a state of planetary emergency", which will "unless halted and reversed with immediate effect [...] cause significant damage to global economy, social and political resilience and stability and will render the Sustainable Development Goals impossible".[2] With laudable exceptions meaningful action falls short, let alone "with immediate effect".[3]

---

[*] This article is based on the lecture given at the opening of the research center ClimLaw: Graz but has been revised and extended for the purpose of this publication.

[1] Olivier Moréteau, Le droit commun outil de gestion citoyenne des biens communs maritimes et terrestres p. 16 (not yet published); the text quoted says (my colloquial translation): to obtain a snowball effect, one has to throw the first snowball before the snow has disappeared because of climate change.

[2] Leaders' Pledge for Nature, www.leaderspledgefornature.org/. As usual, the laudable pledge is confined to rather vague measures. That is not to say that such pledges are unimportant; that goes in particular for setting "clear and robust targets, underpinned by the best available science and technology, research [...]". They contribute to, if not signal, the (emerging) *opinio juris*, which can be used by courts to colour/interpret vague legal concepts. As to the evergreen of 'indigenous and traditional knowledge': that it is not irrelevant. But the reference sounds too much as the usual compilation required to reach international agreement. In the past such pledges and declarations, however sincere at the time of writing, rarely received a meaningful follow-up, apart from reformulated new pledges and declarations. They are, in a sense, the only functioning *perpetuum mobile*. The pledge also contains a new feature: "redouble our efforts to end traditional silo thinking", not unimportant because the earlier – often unnoticed – doubling was quite ineffective.

[3] The leaders rightly observe that "the global trends continue rapidly in the wrong direction", but do not ask themselves: how come? To avoid any misunderstanding, it would be unfair to put all the blame on them. But it would be mistaken to believe that they are not part of the problem. *See* extensively the sobering UN

To the best of my knowledge, for the first time, the leaders "commit [...] not simply to words, but to meaningful action [...]. It marks a turning point [...]".[4] It would be a turning point indeed.

This being said, however, it is easy to blame others. The reality is that even people like me, who work, so to speak, 24/7 to stem the tide, find it difficult to practice their own gospel. Most of us could live a more sustainable life or could have fully respected COVID-19 measures imposed or advocated by our governments.

At some stage, the virus will disappear. Climate change is doomed to worsen.[5] We may already have lost battles, but we can still win the war (to keep global warming below fatal thresholds). To that effect, it is of utmost importance to focus on what can and must be done *right now*. More likely than not, our goals (dreams, if you like) will not be fulfilled. Yet together we can make a difference.

We must *also* start thinking about how to cope with the challenges posed by climate change if society is going to waste, once again, vital years. First and foremost: how far can the law be stretched in formulating far-reaching legal obligations to avert catastrophe? In the short term, such obligations will have a major adverse impact on many people and the global economy. Far-reaching measures in affluent countries will also jeopardise poor countries because tourism and export of their products will decrease. Exploring strategies to stem the tide inevitably requires an awkward balancing of inter- and intragenerational interests. This balancing effort may put significant stress on democracy, irrespective of the choices to be made.

In – not unrealistic – doom scenarios, adaptation will pop up. Adaptation is about more than building dykes and the best possible protection against the adverse consequences of climate change, such as hurricanes and droughts. It is also about massive migration, a very sensitive issue that will become a reality sooner than later. These thorny issues will not be discussed in this article; they are huge and important topics in their own right.

---

environment programme, Emissions Gap Report 2020, www.unep.org/emissions-gap-report-2020, in particular executive summary p. vii ff.

4   Pledge under 10.

5   *See* in considerable detail Principles on Climate Obligations of Enterprises, 2nd ed. (EP), Eleven Publishing 2020, also available at www.climateprinciplesforenterprises.org p. 28 ff and UN Environment Programme et al., The Production Gap, 2019 Report, www.unep.org/resources/report/production-gap-report-2019. As climate change is inextricably linked to biodiversity, keeping climate change below fatal thresholds is a double catch. The EU Green Week of 2020 emphasised the interlinkage; *see* EU Commission, New Beginning for People and Nature, EU Green Week Puts the Spotlight on Nature as Our Strongest Ally in Green Recovery (https://ec.europa.eu/environment/news/eu-green-week-puts-spotlight-nature-our-strongest-ally-green-recovery-2020-10-16_en). *See* for a more optimistic note Lucy Colback, The Role of Business in Climate Change, FT Future Forum, 18 December 2020, www.ft.com/content/7ab0bfb0-b37c-463d-b132-0944b6fe8e8b.

2   Lessons to Be Learned From the COVID-19 Crisis

The COVID-19 crisis adds new challenges to the debate about climate change. The amounts of public money spent to help immediate victims of the COVID-19 crisis and the resulting skyrocketing national debts in many countries, which will have to be repaid at some stage, could well be (felt as) a hurdle to taking effective measures to come to grips with climate change.[6]

One cannot escape the impression that the COVID-19 crisis is suboptimally handled in many countries. With a few notable exceptions, that is indisputably true of climate change. The responses made by the international community, governments and the corporate world have in common: they are too late and too few. There are many reasons for this regrettable state of affairs, a few of which are listed here:

- democracy, in the famous words of Churchill: "the worst form of government, except for all the others", is seemingly inapt for major crises;[7]
- interrelated with the first bullet point: politicians' room for manoeuvre is limited if 'the public' does not support harsh measures that need to be taken. That, I think, is one of the reasons why politicians often shy away from taking painful measures at a stage where the significant adverse consequences of a sit-and-wait position are not (yet) clearly visible to the people (their voters), even though the problem could still have been solved at an early stage at relatively modest costs. In this respect, COVID-19 brings us an alarming message. Quite understandably, most people have great difficulty accepting major restrictions if there is no light at the end of the tunnel.

That problem is magnified in the case of climate change. Even if global emissions could be reduced to zero overnight – a phantom, of course – climate change will worsen owing to the impact of past greenhouse gas (GHG) emissions. Perhaps, at some stage, we will be able to return to an increase of less than 1°C compared with pre-industrial times. In the meantime, humankind, nature and the economy will have paid a high toll. Taking timely bold measures saves substantial costs and avoids the deleterious consequences of unabated climate change. That, however, is not visible, forming the perfect basis for part of the

---

6   The leaders' pledge cited in footnote 2 contains the assurance "that our response to the current crisis is green and just", and "commit putting [inter alia] climate [...] at the heart of our COVID-19 recovery strategies and investments and of our pursuit of national and international development and cooperation". Let us keep our fingers crossed.

7   *See,* about the political impotence, Corey J.A. Bradshaw, Paul R. Ehrlich et al., Underestimating the Challenges of Avoiding a Ghastly Future, www.frontiersin.org/articles/10.3389/fcosc.2020.615419/full pp. 5 and 6.

ultra-right-wing press to treat their readers on messages not based on science.[8] Their stories fuel radicalisation of the political spectre.

Last but not least, in a decade or so, climate science has made impressive progress, yet many vital uncertainties persist: when will tipping points be passed; how high can the sea level be expected to rise in a specific scenario and by when; what means of effectuating negative emissions will become available, by when and at what cost?[9] That means that politicians, the corporate sector and lawyers (courts included) have to base their 'reaction' on insufficient knowledge, although I quite strongly believe that they have often had enough knowledge to understand that much more had to be done.[10]

So much is clear: the window of time available to take steps to avoid global catastrophe at an affordable price is swiftly closing. Every wasted year will require more draconian additional measures, making it even more of a challenge to gain public support.

3   The Way Ahead

If the corona crisis has taught us anything, it is that we need to act swiftly and decisively. If the world that we have 'created' is capable of coping with the unprecedented challenge of climate change, 'we' must do the following:

1. Convey the message of what needs to be done, why that is necessary, and why the proposed measures strike the right balance between and within generations (the inter- and intragenerational equity feature). We need to involve experts in communication, sociology and psychology to tailor the message to the relevant audience.[11]
2. Try as hard as we can to put our cards in the most effective and cheapest measures. That may sound self-explanatory, but it is not. I.e., renewable energy will often be much

---

8   Even a recently appointed US Supreme Court justice casts doubts about climate change: Jeffrey D. Sachs, Amy Coney Barrett Showed She's Ready to be Part of Trump's Post-truth Strategy, www.jeffsachs.org/newspaper-articles/8x9btnsazlta5nfxw8bkbefbks23nc.

9   *See* in extensively, also for references, Commentary to the Principles on Climate Obligations of Enterprises, 2nd ed., *id,* section 7.

10   *See* for other relevant issues the IMF, World Economic Outlook, October 2020, A Long and Difficult Ascent, www.imf.org/en/Publications/WEO/Issues/2020/09/30/world-economic-outlook-october-2020.

11   That will be quite a challenge. Intrusive messages by the IPCC, UN environment programme and others do not eventuate the necessary steps; *see* i.e. Emissions Gap Report 2020, *id.* p. vii ff. Part of the story may be that their messages are clear and compelling but do not point to sufficiently concrete measures to be taken by specific States (and enterprises). If our times and history have taught us anything, it is that it is possible to gain support for specific ideas, albeit that the ideas that have gained support/appealed to 'people' have often had disastrous consequences. Let us try to gain support for useful ideas! Bradshaw et al., *id.* p. 8 add that "[g]iven the existence of a human 'optimism bias' that triggers some to underestimate the severity of a crisis and ignore expert warnings, a good communication strategy must ideally undercut this bias without inducing disproportionate feelings of fear and despair".

more effective and cheaper compared with isolating old houses. This is not a time for hobby horses.

3. The better strategy is probably to get a major part of the job done by the corporate sector. This does not imply that it is the one and only, or even the most important, source of global emissions.[12] The argument rests on pragmatic and realistic considerations. The corporate sector is in a position to effectuate a significant part of the global reductions by curbing its own emissions, selecting the least carbon-emitting suppliers and reducing the carbon footprint of its products and services. Most electricity suppliers can switch to renewable energy. Enterprises are often in a position to add their costs to the price of their products and services.[13]

My expectation is that this approach will gain acceptance without much ado. Ultimately, people will have to pay the price anyway by means of taxes, levies and measures they are bound to achieve themselves or higher prices for products and services, or, in case of business as usual, by paying the colossal price of unabated climate change. This approach makes the costs less visible, thereby (hopefully) helping to avert fierce resistance.

4 Ambition and Reality: Climate Science and the Political Arena

The UN Framework Convention on Climate Change of 1992[14] put climate change on the map. The IPCC Fourth Assessment Report of 2007 emphasised the need to keep climate change below 2°C.[15] The Paris Agreement (PA)[16] was a milestone but not the game changer many hoped it would be.

Already in 2009 , the Commonwealth Climate Change Declaration labelled climate change "the predominant global challenge". The heads of government discussed their "profound concern about the undisputed threat that climate change poses to the security, prosperity, economic and social development of our people".[17] Ten years later, at the Conference on Parties (COP) in Madrid, the evergreens pop up again:

---

12 Unless one would attribute all emissions in subsequent chains to the enterprise that put a specific product on the market; that stance is not taken in the EP; *see* commentary to the 2nd ed. p. 60 ff.

13 *See also* Emissions Gap Report 2020 p. 62 ff.

14 What is the United Nations Framework Convention on Climate Change? https://unfccc.int/process-and-meetings/the-convention/what-is-the-united-nations-framework-convention-on-climate-change.

15 www.ipcc.ch/site/assets/uploads/2018/02/ar4_syr_spm.pdf.

16 The Paris Agreement, https://unfccc.int/process-and-meetings/the-paris-agreement/the-paris-agreement.

17 The Commonwealth, Commonwealth Declarations, https://thecommonwealth.org/sites/default/files/inline/Commonwealth_Declarations_070619.pdf p. 69.

8. Re-emphasizes with *serious concern* the *urgent need* to address the *significant* gap between the aggregate effect of Parties' mitigation efforts in terms of global annual emissions of greenhouse gases by 2020 and aggregate emission pathways consistent with holding the increase in the global average temperature to well below 2°C above pre-industrial levels and pursuing efforts to limit the temperature increase to 1.5°C above pre-industrial levels.[18]

The 'serious concern' is expressed by those who fell short.[19] Over the years, there has been a huge gap between laudable intentions, often cast in flowery language and action. Until very recently, global emissions were rising; the corona crisis has temporarily changed that trend.[20] The only positive effect of the COVID-19 crisis is that a downward emission trend may continue for a while.[21] Even if global emissions decreased from now onwards, these reductions would likely fall significantly short of keeping the increase in global temperature bearable.[22]

If words equated to action, solutions would be within reach. Mere intentions, however valuable and genuine, do not solve problems.

5   THE LEGAL ARENA

A series of authoritative reports, judgments and academic writings tackle a myriad of aspects of climate change. For now, much territory is uncharted.

5.1   *Hopeful Developments*

To begin with, a few hopeful developments occurred in the legal arena. In September 2019, five UN human rights treaty bodies issued a powerful joint statement on human rights

---

18   UN Climate Change Conference – December 2019 UNFCCC Decision 1 https://unfccc.int/cop25. *See* about the increasingly alarmist language Ben Boer, The University of Sydney Law School Legal Studies Research Paper Series, No. 20/25, April 2020, The Preamble, http://www.austlii.edu.au/au/journals/USydLRS/2020/13.pdf p. 7 ff.

19   By 'those' I mean the legal entities. The people at the wheel were often different, but few of the newcomers have shown more eagerness than their predecessors to translate words into meaningful action.

20   *See* Bloomberg Green, A Pandemic that Cleared Skies and that Halted Cities Isn't Slowing Global Warming, www.bloomberg.com/graphics/2020-how-coronavirus-impacts-climate-change/?srnd=green&utm_source=InsideClimate+News&utm_campaign=9010df9055-&utm_medium=email&utm_term=0_29c928ffb5-9010df9055-327952769.

21   *See* Zhu Liu, Philippe Cais, Zhu Deng et al., Near-Real Monitoring of Global CO2 Emissions Reveals the Effects of the COVID-19 Pandemic, https://rdcu.be/b9l1Z.

22   *See,* for elaboration the commentary to the 2nd ed. to the EP, p. 28 ff and the Emissions Gap Report 2020, *id.* p. xi ff.

and climate change.[23] The statement emphasised, inter alia, the importance of keeping climate change below 1.5°C, adding that

> adverse impacts on human rights are already occurring at 1°C of warming and every additional increase in temperatures will further undermine the realization of rights.[24]

Senior members of the judicial community have issued statements and delivered promising presentations, mostly in the context of human rights or the protection of the environment. There is no valid reason why their view would be any different in relation to climate change. A few examples may be noted:

- Laurent Fabius, the President of the French Constitutional Council (the highest court of the country): we must rise to the key challenges of our time, or risk being destroyed by them;[25]
- Guido Raimondi, the then President of the European Court of Human Rights (ECtHR): [t]hroughout this sixty years period [of its existence], the Court[26] has interpreted the convention dynamically in the light of living conditions, which have evolved considerably. Europe in the 1950s and the world we now live in are very different places. Our ways of life and moral standards are no longer the same;[27]

---

23 www.ohchr.org/en/NewsEvents/Pages/DisplayNews.aspx?NewsID=24998&LangID=E and for elaboration on the human rights in point the introduction under 3.

24 Introduction under 5. *See also* Safe Climate, A Report of the Special Rapporteur on Human Rights and the Environment, https://wedocs.unep.org/bitstream/handle/20.500.11822/30158/Safe_Climate_Report. pdf?sequence=1&isAllowed=y.

25 Speech on 25 January 2019 at the European Court of Human Rights' www.echr.coe.int/Documents/Speech_20190125_Fabius_JY_ENG.pdf.

26 This seemingly includes the former Commission. *See,* for the role courts could play, Christina Voigt and Zen Makuch (eds), Courts and the Environment.

27 Opening speech on January 25, 2019 at the European Court of Human Rights, www.echr.coe.int/Documents/Speech_20190125_Raimondi_JY_ENG.pdf. The Tunis Declaration, Universal-ICJ-The-Tunis-Declaration-Advocacy-2019-ENG.pdf, puts it as follows: "the Rule of Law is [...] necessarily a normative concept, consisting of principles and correlative standards and subject to progressive development" (under 3); *see also* Antonio Herman Benjamin, We, the Judges, and the Environment, 29 Pace Envtl. L. Rev. 582 (2012) and Robert Carnwath, Human Rights and the Environment, www.supremecourt.uk/docs/speech-190620.pdf: "To me as an environmental lawyer and judge, the crucial point is that we have more than political commitments or even general human rights protections. We have a strong legal framework, with clear and enforceable precise targets based not on independent expert advice. We need to direct all our efforts to achieving comparable legal regimes across the globe" (p. 14). *See also* Jaap Spier, Mistake of Law and Sustainability, in Ernst Karner et al. (eds), Essays in Honour of Helmut Koziol pp. 163 and 164.

- Justice Brian Preston: In the climate change context, courts have moved beyond their primary function of resolving disputes between private individuals and are now being used by public interest litigants as vehicles for achieving social change.[28]

The European Union Forum of Judges for the Environment issued a Declaration on Environmental Responsibility:[29]

> 1. Signatories to the Declaration acknowledge that sustainable society necessitates social justice. The latter is based on [...] common bearing of social burdens. Further requirements for a sustainable and just society are the preservation and improvement of environmental quality and quality of life, as well as the sustainable use of natural resources [...].
> 2. Signatories to the Declaration consider the protection and representation "of the biosphere and of goods without market value *their pre-eminent task* [...]".

A declaration by the International Union for Conservation of Nature (IUCN) on the Environmental Rule of Law[30] breathes the same spirit, which is all the more important because it is (almost) literally taken over from a Declaration adopted by top judges at a gathering in Rio de Janeiro:[31]

> Foundations of the Environmental Rule of Law
> The environmental rule of law is understood as the legal framework of procedural and substantive rights and obligations that incorporates the principles of ecologically sustainable development in the rule of law. Strengthening the environmental rule of law is the key to the protection, conservation, and restoration of environmental integrity. Without it, environmental governance and the enforcement of rights and obligations may be arbitrary, subjective, and unpredictable.

---

28 Brian J. Preston, Characteristics of Successful Environmental Courts and Tribunals, http://www2.law.mercer.edu/elaw/environmental%20courts.pdf p. 36.
29 www.eufje.org/images/docConf/bud2014/Declaration_environmental_responsibility.pdf.
30 www.iucn.org/sites/dev/files/content/documents/english_world_declaration_on_the_environmental_rule_of_law_final.pdf.
31 I had the honour to participate.

There are also a few stunning judgments, such as

- Urgenda[32] (injunctive relief to the effect that the State of the Netherlands has to reduce its GHG emissions by 2020 by at least 25% compared with 1990);
- a judgment of the Land and Environment Court of New South Wales: there is no room for a new coal mine.[33]

5.2   *Damages: The New Focus?*

Damages, remediation and access to justice have long occupied the attention of the drafters of international instruments[34] mostly in the context of impairment of the environment and violation of human rights.[35]

---

32 Hoge Raad 20 December 2019, ECLI:NL:HR:2019:2006 and for an unofficial translation in English ECLI:NL:HR:2019:2007; about this judgment Jaap Spier, Netherlands International Law Review (NILR) Vol. 67 Number 2 – 2020. *See* for a somewhat similar judgment Conseil d'Etat (19 November 2020) Grande-Synthe and a judgment of the Tribunal administratif de Paris, 3 February 2021 (Association Oxfam France et al.), Tribunal administratif de Paris : L'affaire du siècle (http://paris.tribunal-administratif.fr/Actualites-du-Tribunal/Communiques-de-presse/L-affaire-du-siecle). In his dissenting opinion in *Chernaik v. Brown*, Chief Justice Walters, of the Supreme Court of Oregon, takes the view that "[t]his court can and should issue a declaration that the state has an affirmative fiduciary duty to act reasonably to prevent substantial impairment of public trust resources", 367 Or 143 (2020) at 170, adding "time is now" (at 171); "(o)ne of the core functions of the judicial branch is to determine the legal authority and obligations of the other two branches of government" (at 177 with elaboration); "the applicable standard is objective reasonableness" (at 181), which requires balancing of competing interest (at 185); "[h]ow best to address climate change is a daunting question with which the legislative and executive branches of our state government must grapple. But that does not relieve our branch of its obligation to determine what the law requires" (at 187). *See also* Irish Supreme Court in Friends of the Irish Environment and The Government of Ireland, http://blogs2.law.columbia.edu/climate-change-litigation/wp-content/uploads/sites/16/non-us-case-documents/2020/20200731_2017-No.-793-JR_opinion.pdf. In *Dini Ze' v. Canada*, Federal Court, 6 November 2020, 2020 FC 1059, the claim was held non-justiciable: the "issue of climate change, while undoubtedly important, is inherently political, not legal, and it is of the realm of the executive and legislative branches of the government" at 77 and, in more detail17-76.

33 *Gloucester Resources v. Minister for Planning*, www.caselaw.nsw.gov.au/decision/5c59012ce4b02a5a800be47f.

34 *See* in more detail, also for further references, my Shaping the Law for Global Crises: Thoughts about the Role the Law Could Play to Come to Grips with the Major Challenges of Our Time p. 181 ff; Injunctive Relief: Opportunities and Challenges: Thoughts About a Potentially Promising Vehicle to Stem the Tide, in Jaap Spier and Ulrich Magnus (eds), Climate Change Remedies p. 21 ff, Liability for Climate Change Losses: A Blessing or a Curse, in Frits-Joost Beekhoven van den Boezem, Corjo Jansen and Ben Schuijling (eds), Sustainability and Financial Markets p. 59 ff and Private Law as a Crowbar for Coming to Grips with Climate Change, KNVIR 2018 p. 25 ff, in particular p, 47 ff; Martin Spitzer and Bernhard Butscher, Liability for Climate Change: Cases, Challenges and Concepts, 2 JETL (2017) p. 137 ff and Monika Hinteregger, Civil Liability and the Challenges of Climate Change: A Functional Analysis, 2 JETL 238 ff. (2017).

35 *See* Strategies to Keep Global Warming Below 2 Degrees and to Avoid Devastating Liability, Prepared for the PRI in Person Conference, San Francisco 2018, https://custom.cvent.com/A7020F0F9A8247B2A60 95E2EF0DC7D77/files/Event/5a2f15d64e534edb8f77813a1c7eb7de/cb1ae2a16cb54bb7a913403abf02e219.pdf. *See* in the German context extensively Wagner/Arntz, Nitsch, Habersack/Ehrl, Duve/Hamama, Kahl/Stürmlinger in Kahl/Weller (eds), Climate Change Litigation p. 405 ff and about the Polluter Pays Principle Rehbinder, in Kahl/Weller, *id.* p. 45 ff and in the Indian fascinating context Lovleen Bhullar, The

Access to justice is one of the key elements of human rights law[36] and its slipstream the OECD Guidelines for Multinational Enterprises.[37] Naturally, access to justice does not mean that claims have to be honoured. That is self-explanatory if they are ill-founded. It is far less obvious if they have merit.

The borderline between access to justice and an obligation to 'remediate' harm is not overly clear.[38] One can debate at length whether hurdles to remediation based on legal doctrine (say minimal contribution/'drop in the sea' of a specific violation of human rights in the realm of climate change) or judicial policy (i.e. keeping the floodgates shut) are reconcilable with the idea that justice must be done in case of a violation of human rights or impairment of the environment. Whether one likes it or not, justice is a flexible concept that does not equate to the interests of (potential) victims, however important. As a matter of fact, each human activity has an impact on the environment and on the living conditions of people. Each emission, each flight, each consumption of coffee or meat has an adverse impact on the climate; major factories tend to emit a lot. That does not mean that these activities are necessarily a violation of human rights or a *legally* relevant impairment of the environment. One has to first sort out the point at which the borderline between lawful and unlawful is crossed.

The legal terminology used in a specific legal instrument, be it a convention, treaty or soft law document, may determine the fate of claims for damages. I.e., the use of the word 'remediation' may not be *meant* as creating compensation rights, let alone fully-fledged compensation for all thinkable losses caused by the violation of a human right or impairment of the environment. It leaves room for courts and tribunals to interpret the word narrowly, or extensively. Hence, it would be desirable to explicitly and clearly define what crucial terms aim to say, if not for other reasons, for allowing potential perpetrators to anticipate the potential legal consequences of their acts and omissions.[39] Alternatively, the relevant instruments, or a commentary thereto, could emphasise that they do not aim at remediation or compensation for climate losses or that they do so only in exceptional cases.

Polluter Pays Principle: Scope and Limits of Judicial Decisions, Shibani Ghosh (ed.), Indian Environmental Law p. 152 ff.

36 Dinah Shelton, Remedies in International Law (3rd ed.) pp. 17, 18, 57, 58, 70, 72 and 96-100.

37 *See* under IV.6; "legitimate processes in the remediation of adverse human rights impacts".

38 *See,* for elaboration, Dinah Shelton, *id.* pp. 16 ff and 89 ff. *See,* for the procedural aspects of access to justice in an environmental context, Jona Razzaque, Human Rights to a Clean Environment: Procedural Rights, in Malgosia Fitzmaurice, David M. Ong and Panos Merkouris (eds), Research Handbook on International Environmental Law p. 284 and in the same book Phoebe Okawa, Responsibility for Environmental Damage p. 303 ff, Louise Angéliqie de la Fayette, International Liability for Damage to the Environment p. 320 ff and Amanda Perry-Kessaris, Corporate Liability for Environmental Harm p. 361 ff.

39 That also goes for terminology such as 'the environment' and 'sustainable development'; *see,* about the latter, Nico Schrijver, The Evolution of Sustainable Development in International Law: Inception, Meaning and Status, in particular p. 208 ff.

Occasionally (draft) legal instruments open the door to a wider range of claims.[40] By way of example, the EU is currently contemplating creating an "intrinsic right to nature" and compensation of "pure ecological harm".[41]

However appealing liability may be to (alleged) victims, it does not contribute to what should be our first and foremost priority: prevention. Worse, far-reaching liability in the realm of climate change causes more problems than it solves. The ill-considered claims by some US plaintiffs against the oil majors – regardless their legal and moral basis – illustrate that point.[42] The plaintiffs turn things upside down. The capacity of all enterprises and most States to bear alleged losses is limited. I cannot think of any justification why the fruits of liability should be reaped by those who majorly contributed to the climate crisis instead of compensating poor victims and vulnerable countries. That is not any different if the claims are based on allegedly misleading information about the threats of climate change and/or concealing knowledge about these risks. As far back as, at least, the early nineties of the 20th century, the adverse consequences of climate change were common knowledge. They did not serve as an incentive to take adequate action to stem the tide. Thirty years later, that is not significantly different in many countries.

A focus on *environmental* losses further complicates the discussion. In run-of-the-mill cases, compensation of damage to the environment is not problematic. In worst-case scenarios, it may end up in the bankruptcy of one or a few defendants; that does not stir the world. Climate change is a different issue altogether.

That begs terribly difficult questions, not typically of a legal nature: moral plays a role in shaping the law. To what extent are we (is 'the law') willing to compensate losses to 'nature'? Should such compensation get priority over losses (including the costs of adaptation) of, say, poor people or vulnerable countries? How much should be left to future victims? Posing these questions is easy; answering them is not. There is no self-explanatory answer. That reinforces the urgent need to give these questions serious thought.

---

40   See the definition of 'victim' in Art. 1 of the OEIGWG Chairmanship second revised draft of 6 August 2020, 7ebffa2b7510a719d61fdab83fd8b2c19de4c650.pdf (https://media.business-humanrights.org/media/documents/7ebffa2b7510a719d61fdab83fd8b2c19de4c650.pdf). Art. 2 speaks of 'any harm', whereas Art. 8 para 1 requires State parties to ensure "a comprehensive adequate system of legal liability"; Art. 4 para 2 under guarantees the right to access to justice and "effective remedy in accordance with [...] international law, such as [...] compensation, [...] environmental remediation and ecological restoration"; see, about access to remedy, Art. 7 and, about 'legal liability', Art. 8. A third revised version was published after submission of this contribution.

41   See my presentation at the EU Green Week October 2020, https://climateprinciplesforenterprises.org/presentation-of-prof-dr-jaap-spier-eu-green-week/.

42   See Oil Majors Gear Up for Wave of Climate Change Liability Lawsuits, Financial Times (www.ft.com/content/d5fbeae4-869c-11e9-97ea-05ac2431f453). In a not overly considered document titled Why and How Investors Should Act on Human Rights, www.unpri.org/human-rights-and-labour-standards/why-and-how-investors-should-act-on-human-rights/6636.article, UN PRI seems to promote liability of investors that contributed or are directly linked to 'negative outcomes' of their investment decisions for 'people affected'. The document begs many questions.

We desperately need to map a sound, fair and balanced trajectory for compensating climate losses, present and future.[43] Crushing liability should not be the answer. A collapse of the global economy is unavoidable if we open the floodgates; not overnight, but it is just a matter of time.[44] With the exception of the super-rich, such a collapse will jeopardise people around the globe, rich and poor. As so often happens, the most serious consequences will be felt by the most vulnerable people who already live on or below the poverty line.

This presupposes that liability is not a non-starter from scratch. Causation is probably the major hurdle. The minimum contribution of most states and enterprises to climate losses around the globe is a legal hurdle that can be removed.[45] It may be a bit of a challenge to prove that a specific loss is caused by climate change. Take, for instance, a drought. It may be caused by climate change; it might also have occurred anyway. That problem can easily be solved by the doctrine of proportional liability if a court would be willing to grant compensation.

The real trick lies in the calculation of a specific defendant's contribution to global climate change. Ahrens contends that – under German law – there is no causation if the damage is too diffuse, i.e. the loss stems from indistinguishable emissions from a great many sources.[46] Ahrens has a point. Current emissions produce the full effect only after one or a few decades. That makes it very difficult to determine the contribution of a specific emission to a specific loss. That problem is exacerbated in the case of continuing emissions that change over time. In that respect, proportional liability poses gigantic challenges. How to determine the proportion? Do all or only wrongful global emissions count? Relevant information will probably be available about the perpetrator. But is it also in relation to all wrongful emissions of the corporate world? Probably not. Even if the information were traceable, the calculation would be a nightmare.

Probably, the only 'solutions' to the problem signalled by Ahrens are working with ballpark figures and magic words. In my 19 years in the Supreme Court, I have learned that magic words are surprisingly convincing to most lawyers and others.

Just mentioned challenges are a blessing in disguise to those who are keen to avoid any liability for climate losses, as I have been advocating for years.[47] Seeing the blatant

---

43 *See,* for elaboration, J. Spier, KNVIR, *id.* p. 47 ff and in Beekhoven van den Boezem et al., *id.* p. 75 ff, also for further references.

44 W. Kahl and M-P Weller contend that "if the first courts believe that threshold of causality can be overcome" this "would certainly be a "watershed" of considerable magnitude for the doctrine of private law but would also entail considerable financial consequences (liability risks) for the major CO2 emitters in the corporate sector", in Kahl/Weller, *id.* p. 559. The implications of such judgments will depend on the number of courts that would adhere to such a view, whether these courts would arrive at the conclusion of far-reaching liability (including the scope of damages) and whether their judgments are enforceable against many enterprises. If all that would happen, 'considerable financial consequences' is quite an understatement.

45 *See* the commentary to the updated EP p. 202 ff, also for further references.

46 Quoted by S. Nitsch, in Kahl/Weller, *id.* p. 444.

47 *See* i.e. my Shaping the Law for Global Crises p. 181 ff.

unwillingness of most States and enterprises to curb their emissions significantly for many years, and even these days, the unwillingness to even think about their legal obligations, I no longer believe that liability should be a non-starter *irrespective of the circumstances*. It would be unduly harsh to leave *all* victims empty-handed for losses knowingly caused by affluent countries and major enterprises in those countries. I reiterate that we need an in-depth debate on the question of which victims and which losses should be compensable without running the risk of opening the floodgates, which would mean, inter alia, that future victims will be bereft of compensation.

One cannot escape the impression that drafters of international instruments do not always realise the potential consequences of the texts of their instruments.[48] The common denominator of – on paper – highly ambitious instruments, or instruments with a very broad scope, is that the drafters lump too much together. Child labour, pollution of a river, destruction of the culture of native populations require a different stance compared with global issues such as climate change. Far-reaching compensation will often be desirable and manageable in relation to the former three topics; it is not in relation to climate change. Even more importantly, let us, please, focus predominantly on what matters most: prevention.

5.3   *Litigation: Urgent Need for 'the Right Cases'*

The window of time to keep the increase in global temperature well below 2°C is swiftly closing. Seeing the stalemate in the international political arena and the insufficient ambition of most enterprises, widespread litigation is unavoidable to stem the tide. It may (will) not solve the entire problem, but it could significantly contribute to the almost universally adopted goal to avert global catastrophe.

This requires a global strategy geared towards exploring the most promising and most effective litigation before the 'right' courts. Unlike what some non-governmental organisations (NGOs) seem to believe, 'promising' does not necessarily equate to 'effective'. The chances of obtaining a favourable judgment in a trivial case may be significant, but that is of limited avail to the climate. In that scenario, the efforts and the money could have been spent more strategically. I cannot escape the impression that quite a few NGOs are predominantly after quick successes that put them in the spotlight. The *world* would be better served with a focus on cases that could have a relevant impact on shaping the law concerning key issues and on the behaviour of States, enterprises and other key players.

---

48   In specific cases the reason may be that the text is a compromise.

5.4   Unfortunate Decisions

Unfortunately, quite a few recent judgments in the realm of climate change ended up in victories for the defendants,[49] although at times judges acknowledged the challenges posed by climate change, occasionally in eloquent language. The Juliana case is an example par excellence:

> In the mid-1960s, a popular song warned that we were "on the eve of destruction." The plaintiffs [...] presented compelling evidence that climate change has brought that eve nearer.[50]

A Norwegian production licence for petroleum on the Norwegian Continental Shelf was challenged by Greenpeace on alleged incompatibility with the Constitution of Norway and Articles 2 and 8 ECHR. The Borgarting Court of Appeal emphasises that "the severity of the environmental harm will [...] be the key criterion, based on the significance for human health and the productive capacity and diversity of the natural environment" (Art. 112 para 1 of the Constitution). Actual harm is not required; a risk suffices in line with the precautionary principle. It comes down to "what harm remains after measures have been taken". "The societal considerations behind the encroachment on the natural environment and the societal costs of the measures are key." All emissions, both from the production and the combustion – domestically or abroad – carry weight. The Court discussed the impact on Norway and notes that there are currently no large-scale technical solutions available for carbon capture and storage. Norway does not meet its self-imposed target (30% reductions by 2020 compared with 1990); "total reported national contributions are too low to fulfil the Paris Agreement targets". The Court – unrealistically – assumes "a well-functioning emissions allowance trading system". Even though the Court emphasises the urgent need to 'drastically' reduce GHG emissions, it notes that "a country can go a long way towards buying itself out". Without much ado, the Court noted that "increased emissions from the Norwegian Continental Shelf will not affect the total emissions within the sectors required". What follows are unsubstantiated speculations about what might happen concerning Norwegian reductions of GHGs. The Court seems to follow the Baron von Münchhausen process: "the view that there is room for the emissions presumes that measures will be taken to reduce total national emissions that can provide such room." At any rate, possible future emissions related to the production licenses [...] do not bear such

---

importance for the national emissions, when the measures taken are also consolidated, that the threshold under Article 112 has been exceeded.

> [A] gradual phasing-out of Norwegian exports of oil and gas [...] does not necessarily mean that the world's energy requirements as a whole will be covered in a more climate-friendly manner.

In the Court's view, the adverse consequences of the licences and the possible harm ("it cannot be ruled out that these will result in loss of human life") do "not clearly fulfil the requirement for a 'real and immediate risk'". Even if the risk would be "real and immediate", the outcome would be the same for the reasons mentioned in relation to Article 112 Constitution.[51]

The judgment was upheld by the plenary of the Norwegian Supreme Court by 11 against 4 Justices. At the time of writing, an English translation is not available. According to the Supreme Court's press release[52]

> The Supreme Court unanimously found, with emphasis on preceding events and the preparatory works to the constitutional provision, that the clear starting point must be that it is the authorities' task to determine which environmental measures to implement. Article 112 of the Constitution may nonetheless be invoked directly before the courts when it comes to environmental issues that the legislature has not considered.
>
> The Supreme Court found that Article 112 of the Constitution must also be read as a safety valve, even if the Storting (the Parliament, JS) has discussed the case. For the courts to have jurisdiction to set aside a legislative enactment, the Storting must have neglected its duties grossly under Article 112 subsection 3. This must also apply for other Storting resolutions and decisions to which the Storting has consented. The threshold is, therefore, very high.
>
> Due to the strict criterion for review, the Supreme Court found that the royal decree was clearly not invalid based on Article 112 of the Constitution.
>
> The Supreme Court mentioned that a number of general and specific measures had been taken to reduce the national climate emissions – including a carbon tax, investments in renewable energy, grants to technology on carbon capture

---

51   Borrowed from my NILR case note on the Urgenda judgment under 15.1 (p. 337 ff), footnotes omitted. *See*, for the judgment of the Court of Appeal, http://climatecasechart.com/climate-change-litigation/non-us-case/greenpeace-nordic-assn-and-nature-youth-v-norway-ministry-of-petroleum-and-energy/.

52   After submission of this article an English translation of the judgment became available: http://climatecasechart.com/climate-change-litigation/wp-content/uploads/sites/16/non-us-case-documents/2020/20201222_HR-2020-846-J_judgment.pdf.

and storage, grants to green technology, and green adjustment in general, and not least the endorsement of the EU's carbon quota system. When it comes to climate emissions from combustion taking place abroad after Norwegian petroleum export, the Supreme Court found that one must accept that the Storting and the Government base Norwegian climate policy on the distribution of responsibility between states in accordance with international agreements. Here, there is a principle that every state is responsible for combustion on its own territory. Finally, the Supreme Court referred to the strict safety regime on the Norwegian continental shelf implemented to protect against local environmental damage.

A principal issue for the environmental groups was that Norway must take a proportionally larger share of the emissions cuts, both because our petroleum production has caused great emissions and because we have the economic capacity to do so. The groups held that Norway must therefore reduce climate emissions by at least 60 percent within 2030. The environmental groups also argued that until a detailed legal framework and climate accounts are in place, the authorities cannot commence exploration in new areas.

In the Supreme Court's view, a validity action like the present one could not be used to draw up such specific requirements based on Article 112 of the Constitution. The starting point for the courts' assessment in a valid action is the contested decision. The arguments of the environmental groups implied that central parts of the Norwegian petroleum policy, with production and export, would be put to the test. This was outside the scope of what the Supreme Court could consider. [...].

The Supreme Court also unanimously found that the royal decree does not violate Article 93 of the Constitution and Article 2 ECHR on the right to life or Article 102 of the Constitution and Article 8 ECHR on the right to respect for private and family life.

To me, this was a strong case. The outcome is unsatisfactory. First, in regard to the climate, it signals that it cannot be taken for granted that courts will assume responsibility where other parts of the trias politica and the corporate world lean backwards. A recent English case about the construction and operation of two gas-fired generation units[53] underscores that courts might well be reluctant to issue the relief sought; see in more detail under 6.

---

53 *ClientEarth v. Sec of State Business*, [2021] EWCA Civ 43, *Client Earth v. SOS for Business*, Energy and Industrial Stategy judgment (www.judiciary.uk/wp-content/uploads/2021/01/ClientEarth-v-Sec.-of-State-for-business-energy-and-industrial-strategy-judgment.pdf).

Thus, I am not saying that the Supreme Court's arguments do not have any (legal) merit. Rarely are these kinds of cases black or white. I strongly believe that it would have been possible to decide differently. Without courageous judges prepared to break new ground and, if necessary, stretch 'the law' to its outer limits, humanity's future looks bleak.

As will be discussed in what follows, there is an emerging view that there is and should not be room for the exploration of new oil and gas fields. This also seems to be the view of the US Court of Appeals for the Ninth Circuit in *Ctr. For Bio. Diversity v. Zinke*.[54] The Court was not saying and was not asked to say[55] that such explorations should be a no go, but it emphasised that the climate impact must be given genuine weight, the need to consider a "no action alternative"[56] and "the direct and indirect effects of the proposed action".[57]

The most striking example of despair is the announced outcome of a case submitted to the Human Rights Commission of the Philippines: climate change is *not* a human rights issue.[58]

5.5   *Not Overly Considered Claims*

In some cases, the plaintiffs operated on the fringe of what could reasonably be expected from a court. A German plaintiff relied, inter alia, on allegedly binding self-imposed obligations that the court characterised as "eine bunte Broschüre [...] mit vielen Fotos, Abbildungen und Tabellen" (a colourful brochure with many photos, illustrations and tables).[59]

As with many other countries, the Netherlands has provided significant financial support to its national air carrier, KLM (Royal Dutch Airlines), seeing the major adverse impact of the COVID-19 crisis on KLM. Greenpeace sought injunctive relief to the effect that the financial support could be continued only if it were linked to a requirement to

---

54   18-73400.pdf (https://cdn.ca9.uscourts.gov/datastore/opinions/2020/12/07/18-73400.pdf).

55   *See,* for the standard of review, the judgment under IB (p. 10).

56   P. 12 with elaboration on the subsequent pages.

57   P. 16.

58   It was announced at the COP in Madrid (2019!). Ever since, silence has set in. At the time of finalising this contribution (February 2021), to the best of my knowledge nothing has been put on paper. There are different accounts of what Cadiz, allegedly on behalf of the Commission, has said. *See* for diverging impressions: www.ciel.org/news/groundbreaking-inquiry-in-philippines-links-carbon-majors-to-human-rights-impacts-of-climate-change-calls-for-greater-accountability/ and www.climatedocket.com/2019/12/09/philippines-human-rights-climate-change-2/. To the extent I could trace the Commission even refrained from issuing a press release.

59   Verwaltungsgericht Berlin VG 10 K 412.18, www.gerichtsentscheidungen.berlin-brandenburg.de/jportal/por-tal/t/279b/bs/10/page/sammlung.psml?pid=Dokumentanzeige&showdoccase=1&js_peid=Trefferliste&doc-umentnumber=1&numberofresults=1&fromdoctodoc=yes&doc.id=JURE190015283&doc.part=L&doc.price=0.0#focuspoint.

significantly reduce KLM's GHG emissions. As such, the claim is not surprising. All enterprises, including air carriers, should reduce their emissions or at least take countervailing measures.[60] It came as no surprise (to me) that the claim was dismissed. The Court harps on the exceptional circumstances that require a wide margin of appreciation.[61]

To me, this is an example of a case that did not stand a favourable chance from the onset in spite of its *merits*. I am inclined to think that the chance that a court would be prepared to issue the relief sought was limited, seeing the context of an unprecedented challenge to avoid a collapse of the economy. A more promising strategy would have been a focus on a ban on fossil fuel subsidies in general.[62]

A complaint about extradition by New Zealand of a national of Kiribati to his homeland is another example. The applicant argued that he was forced to migrate because of a rise in the sea level. The relevant UN Commission held

> 9.12 In the present case, the Committee accepts the author's claim that sea level rise is likely to render the Republic of Kiribati uninhabitable. However, it notes that the timeframe of 10 to 15 years, as suggested by the author, could allow for intervening acts by the Republic of Kiribati, with the assistance of the international community, to take affirmative measures to protect and, where necessary, relocate its population.[63]

I am not suggesting that this claim did not have merit. The plaintiff ('s lawyer) should have understood, I think, that the Commission had virtually no choice but to dismiss the claim. To put it bluntly, one cannot expect international adjudicators to render judgments that have major ripple effects in a case that, though appealing from the plaintiff's angle, is not serious enough to stir up revolution. That is precisely what a different outcome would have been.[64] Nevertheless, the case should bring the international community to understand that we get ever closer to the fringe of major migration. If the living conditions in specific countries majorly deteriorate, it seems quite possible that other countries are under a legal obligation to cope with these migrants. I know that this is a red herring, but an important

---

60   *See* EP Principle 2.1.1-2.1.4 and about international transport the commentary p. 160 ff.
61   District Court of The Hague 9 December 2020, https://uitspraken.rechtspraak.nl/inziendocument?id=ECLI:NL:RBDHA:2020:12440.
62   *See* the Oslo Principles, Principle 21.
63   https://tbinternet.ohchr.org/_layouts/15/treatybodyexternal/Download.aspx?symbolno=CCPR%2fC%2f127%2fD%2f2728%2f2016&Lang=en.
64   For the avoidance of doubt, I realise what I am saying, and I am not making this point with great enthusiasm. At some stage, arguably sooner than later, affluent countries cannot turn a blind eye to climate refugees. That view, I am afraid, stands a chance of gaining (at least some) acceptance only if the problem has magnified.

one if it could incentivise action to reduce GHG emissions significantly at a much greater pace.

5.6   *Intermediate Category*

The UK Supreme Court (SC) decided a case concerning the framework that will govern an application for the grant of development consent for the construction of a third runway at Heathrow Airport. After a long period of consideration, successive governments have come to the conclusion that there is a need for increased airport capacity in the South East of England to foster the development of the national economy. Such an expansion of airport capacity would involve a substantial increase in CO_2 emissions from the increased number of flights. On 5 June 2018, the Secretary of State laid before Parliament the final version of the airports national policy statement (ANPS), together with supporting documents. The policy framework set out in the ANPS makes it clear that issues regarding the compatibility of the building of a third runway at Heathrow with the UK's obligations to contain carbon emissions and emissions of other GHGs could and should be addressed at the stage of the assessment of an application by Heathrow Airport (HAL) for a DCO (development consent order) to allow it to proceed with the development. The ANPS makes it clear that the emissions obligations to be taken into account at the DCO stage will be those that are applicable at that time, assessed in the light of circumstances and the detailed proposals of HAL at that time. On 25 June 2018, there was a debate on the proposed ANPS in the House of Commons, followed by a vote approving the ANPS by 415 votes to 119, a majority of 296 with support from across the House. On 26 June 2018, the Secretary of State designated the ANPS under section 5(1) of the PA 2008 as national policy.

The lawfulness of the designation of the ANPS was challenged on a wide variety of grounds. The Divisional Court dismissed all the claims. The Court of Appeal granted declaratory relief stating that the ANPS is of no legal effect and that the Secretary of State had acted unlawfully in failing to take into account the PA in making his decision to designate the ANPS. The Court of Appeal added that its

> decision should be properly understood. We have not decided, and could not decide, that there will be no third runway at Heathrow. We have not found that a national policy statement supporting this project is necessarily incompatible with the United Kingdom's required commitment to reducing carbon emissions [...][65]

---

65   Plan B Earth and Secretary of State for Transport Heathrow Airport et al., [2020] EWCA Civ 214, https://www.judiciary.uk/wp-content/uploads/2020/02/Heathrow-judgment-on-planning-issues-27-February-2020.pdf; quote under 285. The description of the case is largely borrowed from the SC's judgement.

The SC allows the appeal on each of its four grounds.[66]

For the purpose of this contribution, I cannot fully discuss the diverging views of the Court of Appeal and the SC. The SC mentions the following balancing factors:

> the National Planning Policy Framework (July 2018), at a very high level the objective of sustainable development involves "meeting the needs of the present without compromising the ability of future generations to meet their own needs"; it has three overarching elements, namely an environmental objective, an economic objective, and a social objective. For a major infrastructure project like the development of airport capacity in the South East, which promotes economic development but at the cost of increased greenhouse gases emissions, these elements have to be taken into account and balanced against each other. Section 10(3)(a) provides that the Secretary of State must, in particular, have regard to the desirability of "mitigating, and adapting to climate change".[67] The SC refers to evidence that the ANPS was "capable of being compatible with the target set by the PA".[68]

The first issue the SC had to deal with (balancing conflicting factors) illustrates that this kind of judgment unavoidably entails value judgments. That makes the outcome of such a case difficult to predict.

The SC's room for manoeuvre is illustrated, I think, by the rather inaccurate reference to 'the target set by the Paris Agreement'. Well below 2°C is hardly a clear target, which means that it is very unclear what the evidence to which the SC refers means to say. In addition: the SC's interpretation of the evidence is certainly not self-explanatory. In these respects, one cannot escape the impression that the Justices were keen to discern arguments to justify their seemingly preferred outcome.[69]

How do these points bear on the question of whether initiating this kind of case is helpful to keep the increase in global temperature below fatal thresholds? Aviation's contribution to climate change is relevant and not covered by the nationally determined contributions (NDCs) under the PA. Based on current trends, aviation and international shipping "are projected to consume between 60 and 220 per cent of allowable CO2 emissions

---

66 R (on the application of Friends of the Earth Ltd and others) (Respondents) v. Heathrow Airport Ltd (Appellant) (www.supremecourt.uk/cases/docs/uksc-2020-0042-judgment.pdf).

67 Under 115. *See*, in the common law context under 116 ff.

68 Under 124. *See* about the influence of the Paris Agreement on litigation Brian J. Preston, The Influence of the Paris Agreement on Litigation: Legal Obligations and Norms, doi 10.1093/jel/eqaa020 and 21, to be published in the Journal of Environmental Law.

69 Some of the other arguments are more convincing to me. In particular, that this was, so to speak, still an early stage of granting permission; *see* under 166.

by 2050 under IPCC illustrative 1.5°C scenarios".[70] Hence, reducing the resulting emissions is important, and even more so is avoiding an increase, which is damaging to the climate. That being said, the answer lies in the grey zone, I am afraid. Undoubtedly, the relevant NGOs did realise that a lot would depend on the Court's appetite to break new ground, not surprisingly seeing the economic interests and the foreseeable criticism from both the government and the public if victory had been granted to the NGOs. They have probably taken into account the potential ripple effect if the case were lost.

Although I have much more sympathy for the Court of Appeal's judgment, the final outcome, though unwelcome, does not come as a complete surprise to me. Other courts had already reached a similar outcome.[71] In the case in point the huge support 'from across the House' of Commons and the political sensitivity of overriding the view of Parliament, particularly in countries such as the UK, does not make it easy for a court to make a diametrically different assessment, even though the UK has adopted the PA and the UK and Northern Ireland's NDC[72] strongly underscores its importance.

Seeing the just mentioned significant future contribution of aviation in depleting the carbon budget, a *reduction* of its carbon footprint is unavoidable. The easiest avenue to achieve that goal is to focus on the emissions of air carriers. If it is not possible to reduce their emissions significantly,[73] they have to reduce the number of flights, which would predominantly affect 1% (!) of the global population.[74]

If a ban on new airports or runways would be a bridge too far for courts (as recent judgments suggest), an alternative approach might be to require airports seeking permission for new runways or other expansions to effectuate stringent measures to reduce their carbon footprint and that of in- and outbound flights. To me, it does not seem overly far-fetched to expect governments considering granting such permissions/permits to urge airports to act along these lines. Such a strategy, although hopefully more promising, is no guarantee of success either. The harsh reality is that courts may have sympathy for such a 'strategy', but shy away from granting judgments that will be outcried as the acme of judicial activism, although, in reality, such judgments would be in the very best public interest, with the exception of the happy few. However, in our wicked world, perceptions, even if nonsensical or very short-sighted, carry much weight.

---

70 Emissions Gap Report 2020, *id.* p. xiii.
71 *See* Friends of the Irish Environment and Fingal County, *Friends of the Irish Environment CLG v. Fingal County Council* – Climate Change Litigation (http://climatecasechart.com/non-us-case/friends-irish-environment-clg-v-fingal-county-council/) and (Austrian) Bundesverwaltungsgericht, 2 February 2017 (Schwechat), http://blogs2.law.columbia.edu/climate-change-litigation/wp-content/uploads/sites/16/non-us-case-documents/2017/20170202_W109-2000179-1291E_decision-2.pdf.
72 The United Kingdom's Nationally Determined Contributions (https://assets.publishing.service.gov.uk/government/uploads/system/uploads/attachment_data/file/943618/uk-2030-ndc.pdf).
73 *See,* for possible options to effectuate reductions, the Emissions Gap Report 2020, *id.* p. 56 ff.
74 Emissions Gap Report 2020 p. 54; *see also* pp. 62 and 63.

An alternative strategy would be to focus predominantly on very promising cases that, if won, could provide guidance/inspiration to other courts. I deliberately formulate cautiously. In borderline cases, it will be difficult to assess ex ante whether a case stands a favourable chance. The Heathrow case was, so to speak, a hard case.

In assessing the chances of success of a case, plaintiffs might be well advised to bear in mind that there are limits to what courts can and are willing to do.[75]

In the coming decade(s), courts will be treated on an increasing number of cases about global issues that are not properly handled by the legislature (both internationally and domestically). It is my hope and, to a slightly lesser extent, expectation that many of them will show courage, that they will assume responsibility to step in where the system fails. Many of these judgments will be decried as the acme of activism, even if they are doing no more than justice to averting global catastrophe. That does not mean that judges will or should close their eyes to such criticism. At the end of the day, judges do not operate in a vacuum. Hence, I would not be surprised if they selectively render ground-breaking judgments. I could imagine and hope that for this purpose they will select cases that could have a measurable impact,[76] particularly so if followed by other courts. Time will tell where the boundaries lie.[77] See for elaboration under 9 below.

5.7 Legal Escapes

Some (perhaps quite a few) judges think *exclusively* in terms of the 'legal system' (doctrine, precedents); to them, that is what the law is about.[78] Others rely on prima facie, far-fetched arguments. For instance, the Superior Court of Quebec in a case in which the plaintiff (Environnement jeunesse) claims that the government fails to put in place the necessary

---

75 In the context of 'willing to do', the obiter in the SC's judgment in the Heathrow case, under 134, is perhaps telling: "In light of the factual position, it is not necessary to decide the different question whether, if the Secretary of State had omitted to think about the Paris Agreement at all […], as an unincorporated treaty, that would have constituted an error of law. *That is not a straightforward issue* and we have not heard submissions on the point. We say no more about it" (emphasis added).

76 I reiterate: that also goes for the expansion of airports. As a matter of fact, most courts will not focus exclusively on the impact on the climate. Personally, I would give priority to the climate to the detriment of the pleasures of increasing travels, realising that air traffic is about more than holidays. The problem can, hopefully, be solved, at least in part, if courageous courts explain in colloquial language/press releases why they render judgments that may not please the public, so to speak.

77 *See,* extensively about this topic, Brian J. Preston, The End of Enlightened Environmental Law, Journal of Environmental Law 2019, https://academic.oup.com/jel/article/31/3/399/5601117?login=true.

78 *See,* i.e., High Court of New Zealand in *Smith v. Fonterra Co-Operative Group Limited,* [2020] NZHC 419 (6 March 2020). No doubt the Court provides a brilliant overview of the key features of tort law, but none of them are compelling to reject the claim, unless one is unwilling to escape from the system (and arguably even within the system). However, the Court creates a small opening: Inchoate duty (under 110 ff).

measures to limit global warming. The court seems quite sympathetic to the claim, but it is dismissed because the 'class' is allegedly arbitrarily composed.[79]

The (in)famous political issue is an(other) easy way out for courts unwilling to assume responsibility for averting global catastrophe.[80] Others may honestly believe that a different judgment would not make any difference, either because the causal contribution of the activity in point is marginal or because others would fill the gap.[81] As to the political issue-doctrine, the approach adopted by the Dutch Supreme Court is much more convincing to me:

> 8.3.2 [...] the government and parliament [...] have a large degree of discretion to make the political considerations that are necessary in this regard. It is up to the courts to decide whether, in availing themselves of this discretion, the government and parliament have remained within the limits of the law by which they are bound.

The Dutch Supreme Court emphasises that in determining the 'limits of the law', regard must be had to the European Convention on Human Rights (ECHR). "The protection of human rights it provides is an essential component of a democratic state under the rule of law."[82]

---

79 Superior Court of Quebec in *Environnement Jeunesse v. Attorney General of Canada*, http://climatecasechart.com/non-us-case/environnement-jeunesse-v-canadian-government/. In such instances empowering NGOs to serve as plaintiffs may help; *see* my presentation at the EU Green Week, October 2020, available at www.climateprinciplesforenterprises.org.

80 *See*, i.e., 'reluctantly' US Court of Appeals for the Ninth Circuit in *Juliana v. United States*; Judge Staton forcefully dissents.

81 As to the latter argument, in the Urgenda case the NGO Urgenda has argued, referring to several reports, including a report by the Danish Council on Climate Change, that, until at least 2050, there are too many ETS rights; the argument was not challenged by the state; *see* the advisory opinion of deputy Procurator-General Langemeijer and Advocate-General Wissink, ECLI:NL:PHR:2019:1026 under 4.208 referring to legal ground 56 of the judgment of the Court of Appeal, which was not challenged in this respect (*see* under 4.210). In other settings the 'waterbed' argument may be true as a matter of fact, at least in the short term. Even in that scenario it should be rejected. If this defence would be honoured, the law cannot offer solace in many cases that truly matter. It would mean tough luck for humanity, the environment and other living species: the law can be of no avail to avert such an evil. Courts unwilling to overcome 'traditional' barriers may honestly believe that this is the one and only decent way to handle cases, but they are mistaken (and I cannot believe that they do not know that). Over the centuries the law has developed. If, for a while, the law is cast in stone, the reason is not 'the law' but the relevant judges' conception of their office.

82 ECLI:NL:HR:2019:2007 under 8.3.3. I realise that the ECHR applies only to countries belonging to the Council of Europe; also that not all regions across the globe have adopted regional human rights instruments. In most instances, there are one or more international instruments that can be invoked. In other instances, the Constitution of the relevant country can offer solace.

5.8   Telling the Fortunes

Time will tell how case law will develop. The famous words of the ECtHR, namely that the law is a living instrument, pave the way for courts keen to change course to overrule precedents or to break new ground. That has happened on many occasions, often to the benefit of society; these judgments were mostly applauded.[83]

To the extent the penny did not (yet) drop, the time has come for courts to realise that they, too, have a role to play. In her dissenting opinion in the Juliana case, judge Staton reminded us

> When the seas envelop our coastal cities, fires and droughts haunt our interiors, and storms ravage everything between, those remaining will ask: Why did so many do so little.[84]

Cautious, or – what in this context comes close – conservative, judges should be reminded that what they are doing is not what they pretend: applying the law in line with what the legislature had in mind. Progressive and conservative judgments have in common that they are based on policy choices, albeit with fundamentally different outcomes.

This being said, some recent cases, such as *Greenpeace v. Norway* and the Heathrow judgment, illustrate that certainly not all, perhaps only quite a few, courts will take up the gauntlet. Some plaintiffs should have realised that the chances of success were slim, noting the stance the relevant courts had taken in other, not necessarily related, cases.

Courts keen to harp on the political argument or (mis)using doctrinal features such as minimum causation to avoid going into the merits of a case are not the most promising battleground for climate cases. In other instances, plaintiffs should *intuitively* understand that victory is unlikely, or at best uncertain. Other cases, again, were not optimally conducted.[85] Another reason could be that the judges are not (yet) convinced that they have a role to play. They may believe that the time has not yet come to enter this politically sensitive scene or may take the view that their judgments will make no difference (a drop in the ocean or the waterbed paradigm).

With the exception of notoriously hopeless courts where litigation should be avoided, plaintiffs would be best advised:
- to explain why their case matters, both from a domestic and from a global angle;
- to explain why they have chosen this case;

---

83   *See*, in more detail, Jaap Spier, The Rule of Law and Judicial Activism: Obstacles for Shaping the Law to Meet the Demands of a Civilized Society, Particularly in Relation to Climate Change, in Michael Faure and André van der Walt (eds), Globalization and Private Law p. 426 ff.

84   *See* footnote 51.

85   I do not want to mention concrete examples, but in some instances it is quite obvious.

- to explain the (potential) impact of a favourable and an unfavourable judgment (the ripple effect);
- to explain why taking a sit-and-wait position is not an option: it is now or never;
- consistently submitting the strongest possible legal, moral and factual bases (however important, not *only* human rights);[86]
- seeking support from experts, international institutions and others whose views might carry weight.

Doing so is no guarantee of victory. Even lost cases may have an impact, if for no other reason than that they (may) bring potential defendants to their senses and (further) activate investors, regulators and supervisory institutions, auditors and credit rating agents. However, too many lost cases are unhelpful.

Courts, reluctant right now for whatever reason, may be willing to leave their self-containment if the penny drops that we are getting closer to global devastation and that they are the last resort. The later the penny drops, the more difficult it will be to stem the tide. That, however, does not mean that judicial 'action' by then will no longer be necessary or welcome. Global devastation will come in degrees. Keeping the increase in global temperature below 2.5°C is preferable compared with 3°C, and 3°C with 4°C.

5.9 Not Only Litigation Matters

Many non-lawyers, most NGOs and (many?) enterprises seem to believe or create the impression that judgments rule the waves in the absence of clear and pertinent legislation or case law. This stance is majorly influenced by the attention 'the press' pays to judgments and litigation.

Needless to say, judgments do matter. First and foremost, they decide a dispute between the parties, if not reversed by a higher court. Judgments by the highest courts have an impact on the law of the land, even if (lower) courts are not (formally) 'bound' by precedent. In the absence of an established 'rule' or precedent, in most instances, courts realise that it is pointless to render judgments that do not stand a chance of being upheld on appeal. If the court concerned has a major stature and/or if the arguments (legal grounds) are convincing, these judgments may contribute to shaping the law in other cases and countries.

However, one should bear in mind that judgments are not delivered in a vacuum. They are not legal reports, academic writings or legislation. They are determined by the facts,

---

86 Cases should also be properly conducted from a procedural angle. Plaintiffs who lost their case should submit as many *relevant* grounds for appeal, which, I am afraid, is not self-explanatory; I could, but do not want to, elaborate on this point. Plaintiffs should not overburden courts with nitty-gritty arguments or trivial issues that detract from the issue at stake.

the arguments of the parties and procedural constraints. The Urgenda case, discussed under 5.1, illustrates that point. The Dutch government had pledged to reduce its emissions by more than the 25% sought by Urgenda.[87] The government could not explain why it had changed its mind nor why 25% would suffice. These facts were not decisive but played a not unimportant role. That limits the 'erga omnes' impact of the SC's judgment, however welcome. In addition, the judgment relies on the ECHR, which does not apply in other parts of the world. Thus, I am by no means suggesting that the judgment cannot serve as a source of inspiration for courts around the globe; I hope it will.

The Norwegian judgment, discussed under 5.4, may not be overly convincing, yet it was rendered, and it is the state of the law in Norway. I guess that it will never be used as a precedent by NGOs. This is understandable, but if they are right that judgments alone, or predominantly, matter, that stance is untenable.

To me it belabours the obvious that not only judgments but also authoritative reports, principles and academic writings can contribute to shaping the law. Because many NGOs contribute to, if not initiate, reports, they seemingly believe that they matter. That being the case, it is not easy to understand why they turn a blind eye to the work of others. Take the Principles on Climate Obligations of Enterprises (EP), endorsed by many distinguished experts; eminent experts kindly wrote supportive prefaces. They are not laws, but the authors' interpretation of the law as it stands or as it will likely develop.[88] One member is a highly respected Australian Justice, while several others held senior judicial offices. Among the endorsers, there are quite a few very senior (retired) members of the judiciary from around the globe. It is very difficult to understand why such principles are less important than a judgment. Make no mistake: that also goes for, *inter alia*, many valuable principles and authoritative reports.

6   LOW-HANGING FRUIT[89]

On a more positive note, it needs to be mentioned that there are quite a few potentially promising[90] legal avenues that could contribute to overcoming the deadlock:

---

87   In the first instance, Urgenda's claim was more ambitious; the court of first instance issued injunctive relief for 25%. Urgenda did not appeal against that judgment, which meant that granting relief for more was a non-starter for the Court of Appeal.

88   Commentary to the 2nd edition p. 70 ff.

89   *See* also the second updated edition of the Principles on Climate Obligations of Enterprises.

90   In each single case potential plaintiffs should meticulously consider whether the case they contemplate initiating stands a favourable chance before the court they have in mind. The diverging stances taken by the Supreme Court of Norway and the US Court of Appeals discussed below illustrate this point. If an NGO would want to challenge, i.e., a new runway, regard should be had to the factors enumerated by the UK Supreme Court in the Heathrow case; *see* under 5.6. To me, a new runway predominantly for outbound holidays is a stronger case to fight compared with inbound tourism, considering the impact on the domestic

- determining the legal obligations of key players.[91] That is what the Oslo Principles (OP) and the Principles on Climate Obligations of Enterprises (EP) have tried to map for respectively States (OP) and enterprises and a few other key players (EP).[92] Most distinguished experts wrote prefaces to the majorly updated second edition of the EP; the UN Special Rapporteur on Human Rights and Environment David Boyd wrote:

> The Principles on Climate Obligations of Enterprises is a timely and compelling book that clarifies the critical role that businesses must play in addressing the global climate emergency and preventing catastrophic impacts on human rights. These principles should be understood and applied as legally binding obligations, not as voluntary guidelines.[93]

---

economy. That is not to say that such a choice reflects my sense of justice, but the question whether a specific case stands a favourable chance is not determined by my preferences.

91   The importance of considering (sic) "what is legally required" is emphasised by Freshfields Bruckhaus Deringer, Business and Human Rights, www.freshfields.com/en-gb/our-thinking/campaigns/biz-human-rights/ p. 5; *see also* pp. 6, 7 and the subsequent pages for country reports. The Climate-Related Market Risk Subcommittee, Market Risk Advisory Committee of the U.S. Commodity Futures Trading Commission, Managing Climate Risk in the U.S. Financial System, CFTC's Climate-Related Market Risk Subcommittee Releases Report, www.cftc.gov/PressRoom/PressReleases/8234-20, is probably right that "disclosure by corporations on material, climate-related financial risks is an essential building block to ensure that climate risks are managed and measured effectively" (p. iv), but it is no more than a building block. A keen understanding of the legal obligations of single enterprises is even more 'essential', also for meaningful disclosure. A judgment issued by the US Court of Appeals for the District of Columbia (*American Lung Association et al v. Environmental Protection Agency*, http://climatecasechart.com/climate-change-litigation/wp-content/uploads/sites/16/case-documents/2021/20210119_docket-19-1140_opinion.pdf), though based on (the interpretation of) US legislation, fuels the submission that all enterprises have reduction obligations; *see,* in particular, p. 37. Understandably, the Court explicitly accepts that "[a]ny regulation of power plants [...] may cause a relative measure in the case of doing business for particular plants and not to others" (p. 89); the EP takes the same approach. Without referring to the EP – she endorsed the first edition – Voigt emphasises the "important role" lawyers have to play "in creating and supporting the legal and regulatory environment for effective implementation" (in Kahl/Weller, *id.* p. 4; *see also* p. 5). She rightly adds that "international standards and goals, can be broken down to national, sub-national and even individual action; that they are easily understandable and, measurable, implementable and reportable" (p. 6). There is no reason why this should be confined to international standards. Most – even august – authors do not go beyond abstract notions about possible legal bases, not showing the slightest interest in making the debate concrete; *see,* i.e., M. Payandeh, in Kahl/Weller, *id.* p. 73/5. I disagree with Payandeh that "[t]he determination of a concrete emission threshold is an inherently political task" (p. 77). I second his view that "[a]lthough the specific content of many international as well as national rules and their implications for climate protection may be open for debate, the indeterminacy of many rules of climate change law does not mean that courts are barred from deciding cases on these rules" (also p. 77).

92   Both published by Eleven International Publishing in, respectively, 2015 and 2018, the second edition in 2020; both the first and the second editions are also available at www.climateprinciplesforenterprises.org under resources.

93   *See* www.climateprinciplesforenterprises.org.

The second edition includes, inter alia, a focus on the obligations of directors. The board should have access to sufficient knowledge, skills and experience to effectively debate and decide on climate-related risks and opportunities.[94] That is no luxury. There is reason to believe that only relatively few "directors sitting on sustainability committees [...] had explicit credentials on sustainability".[95]

At the very least, these Principles, or, if they are challenged, concrete alternative solutions, should be discussed and, if necessary, improved.[96]

It is of significant importance to define obligations as clearly, concretely and unambiguously as possible.[97] Michael Gerrard, one of the world's most active lawyers

---

94 EP Principle 24; *see* for a similar approach Art. 12 of a draft report of the Committee on Legal Affairs of the European Parliament, 2020/2129(INL), PR_INL (www.europarl.europa.eu/doceo/document/JURI-PR-657191_EN.pdf).

95 The Sustainability Board Report 2020, https://a89c8240-f3c4-4e8b-b920-fae532b127b6.filesusr.com/ugd/f6724f_9d0f1b6de2e346a7b0e4fdc163039a98.pdf p. 6. *See* extensively OECD, OECD Due Diligence Guidance for Responsible Business Conduct, https://mneguidelines.oecd.org/OECD-Due-Diligence-Guidance-for-Responsible-Business-Conduct.pdf. According to a statement issued by a series of major enterprises "[s]ome companies already take steps to implement their due diligence processes in line with the corporate responsibility to respect human rights as outlined in the UN Guiding Principles on Business and Human Rights [...]. However, more companies need to take commitments and work to assess, act and report on their potential and actual impacts on human rights and the environment", Business & Human Rights Resource Centre, Support for EU Framework on Mandatory Human Rights and Environmental Due Diligence, www.business-humanrights.org/en/latest-news/support-for-eu-framework-on-mandatory-human-rights-and-environmental-due-diligence/. They "therefore welcome the European Union and its member states' efforts to introduce new mandatory human rights and environmental due diligence legislation". If sufficiently bold, such legislation can only be applauded. It is, however, not a *condicio sine qua non* for due diligence obligations.

96 Some enterprises consider the Science-Based Targets as an alternative; *see* for the (at the time of writing) latest version Foundations for Science-Based Net-Zero Target Setting in the Corporate Sector, https://sciencebasedtargets.org/resources/legacy/2020/09/foundations-for-net-zero-full-paper.pdf. That certainly is a laudable initiative. The EP and the Science-Based Targets have a lot in common. The UN Global Compact, Introducing CFO Principles on Integrated SDG Investments and Finance, foundations-for-net-zero-full-paper.pdf (https://sciencebasedtargets.org/resources/legacy/2020/09/foundations-for-net-zero-full-paper.pdf), also contains valuable recommendations, but its scope is much more limited than the EP. A draft report of the Committee on Legal Affairs of the European Parliament, 2020/2129(INL), PR_INL (www.europarl.europa.eu/doceo/document/JURI-PR-657191_EN.pdf), proposes "non-binding guidelines for undertakings on how best to fulfil the due diligence obligations set out in this directive" (Art. 16). A Resolution of the European Parliament, Texts Adopted – Sustainable Corporate Governance – Thursday, 17 December 2020 (www.europarl.europa.eu/doceo/document/TA-9-2020-0372_EN.html), recommends very similar European legislation on disclosure and governance; it emphasises the need for integrating "sustainability concerns into corporate decision making" (Non-financial reporting obligations under 1); the recitals refer to the EP (mistakenly called Oslo Principles). A joint position of the Alliance for Corporate Transparency emphasises the importance of – inter alia – reporting requirements and governance, Reform_NFRD_Joint_Position_Alliance_for_Corporate_Transparency_final-49dd752b7c4b60a78445a7552004d2d3a3bced19ad48c3072961f9b1eccad53a.pdf.

97 A GRI and USB (University of Stellenbosch Business School) report, Carrots and Sticks, www.usb.ac.za/wp-content/uploads/2020/08/Carrots-Sticks-2020-Report-FIN-21.07.2020.pdf, underscores this view. It contends that "it may be asked whether regulatory requirements for more data disclosures and thematic statements will help to address" the weakness of companies "in reporting quantitative goals and targets, as well as data

---

working on climate change and a member of the Oslo Group, emphasised the need for concretisation as follows: otherwise, it is just as 'send a person to the moon'."[98] To many, that may seems like belabouring the obvious, but the impression is deceptive.

The International Bar Association (IBA) issued a welcome climate crisis statement.[99] It emphasises "that lawyers have an important role to play in addressing the climate crisis". It

> urges lawyers, acting in accordance with their professional conduct rules and the rule of law, to consider (sic): [...] advising clients of the potential risks, liability, and reputational damage arising from activity that negatively contributes to the climate crisis.

Leaving aside the consideration that all activities have an adverse impact on "the climate crisis", the IBA does not address, let alone answer, the vital question, how to assess liability and reputational risks. That is possible only on the basis of a keen understanding of the legal obligations of the clients in point. Perhaps the IBA takes a different stance. More likely than not, the IBA does not *want* to emphasise how important, if not essential, it is for attorneys to discern the legal obligations of their clients in the face of climate change. If my speculation is right, is that reconcilable with "their [members] professional conduct rules"?

The aforementioned second open-ended intergovernmental working group (OEIGWG) draft may serve as another example. Victims shall be guaranteed, inter alia, the right to life (Art. 4 para 2 under b). That may sound self-explanatory because it is the bedrock of human rights treaties and conventions. This crucial right is, however, ambiguous in the context of most sustainability issues, particularly climate change. As a matter of fact, many human activities contribute to the impairment of the right to life. Take GHG emissions.

---

to track progress" p. 30. It is possible to formulate goals, even without a proper understanding of legal obligations. Any goal for the better can only be applauded, but what we need are goals aligned with what the enterprise in point needs to do, which requires an understanding of its legal obligations. Thus, I am by no means suggesting that all kinds of initiatives that promote one or more less concrete trajectories are meaningless. Many of them contain very interesting and valuable ideas; *see,* for a recent example, Terra carta, For Nature, People & Planet, www.sustainable-markets.org/TerraCarta_Charter_Jan11th2021.pdf. They may – and hopefully will – stimulate others to concretise these ideas and to translate them into meaningful action. *See also* IHRB, Just Transitions for All – Business, Human Rights and Climate Action, www.ihrb.org/focus-areas/just-transitions/report-just-transitions-for-all p. 29.

98 The Role of Lawyers in Decarbonizing Society, www.stanfordlawreview.org/online/the-role-of-lawyers-in-decarbonizing-society/.

99 IBA – International Bar Association Climate Crisis Statement (https://www.ibanet.org/MediaHandler?id=822c1967-f851-4819-8200-2fe298164922).

Already at this stage, its death toll is not insignificant,[100] and it will almost certainly majorly increase. Further deterioration can be avoided only if the global community stops emitting GHGs right now. That is a non-starter, from both a practical and legal angle: the excessive burden feature.[101] Hence, we have to explore what level of emissions is, all in all, (legally) 'acceptable'. The appetite for such discussions is very limited,[102] to the detriment of legal certainty, predictability, humankind and the environment.

The view that "carbon emissions are not illegal, i.e. they never were and never will be",[103] is probably more welcome in the ambit of short-sighted people. It is no longer a tenable stance, in light of judgments and authoritative reports from around the globe. Perhaps the proponents of this ludicrous submission meant to say that not all GHG emissions are unlawful, a stance I would second for now.

- litigation against the major worst in class emitters, or enterprises emitting dangerous GHGs such as methane or nitrous oxide;
- a focus on auditors and credit rating agents. They play an important role in the present day's economy. They do not show *any* (visible) interest in the obligations of the auditees or entities they have to rate. Without that knowledge, they cannot properly assess the question of whether or not these entities comply with their obligations, let alone the liability and reputational risk;[104]

---

100 https://time.com/5876229/climate-change-death-rate/ and Climate Change and Health, www.who.int/news-room/fact-sheets/detail/climate-change-and-health. Inconveniently, some measures to cope with climate change entail adverse human rights impacts; *see* also, for concrete examples, IHBR, *id.* p. 22 ff.

101 The better option is that non-excessive or unavoidable emissions (also rather vague criteria) do not amount to a violation of the right to life. According to that reasoning, the formulation of an unqualified right to life, however sympathetic, is misleading. In the context of daily life, the toll of traffic comes at the price of many casualties. No serious plaintiff will argue that states have to bring traffic to a standstill. Balancing exercises are unavoidable; in politics, the (administration of) the law and in moral; *see* i.e. Resolution of the European Parliament on Sustainable Governance, *id.*

102 As already mentioned, the Science Based Targets (SBT) offer an alternative, albeit that it is significantly less detailed compared with the EP and the update; see its version 1.0 of September 2020: Foundations for Science-Based Net-Zero Target Setting in The Corporate Setting. The major differences with the updated version of the EP are that the SBT are based on the need to reduce net anthropogenic emissions to zero by 2050; they allow for betting on technology to effectuate negative emissions. Aki Kachi, Silke Mooldijk, and Carsten Warnecke, Climate Neutrality Claims, How to Distinguish Between Climate Leadership and Greenwashing, https://newclimate.org/2020/09/14/climate-neutrality-claims/, advocate that "[b]oth countries and companies should develop long-term strategies that formulate a decarbonisation pathway which is aligned with scientific knowledge to achieve the temperature limit of the Paris Agreement" (p. 13).

103 G. Wagner and A. Arntz, in Kahl/Weller, *id.* p. 427. I agree with their view that a global solution would be preferable (p. 427/8); they do not use the word 'preferable' but confine themselves to saying that "[g]iven the global scale of the problem, the solution must also be global". In real life that stance implies that we have to accept unheard-off global catastrophes because it is close to unthinkable that such a solution is within reach in the very short time frame still available to ward off catastrophes. Wagner and Arntz fall short of explaining how or why they believe such a solution is going to be forged.

104 *See* Principles 46 and 47 of the updated EP and the commentary thereto p. 285 ff.

- rumour has it that enterprises increasingly seek legal opinions concerning their obligations in the face of climate change. Attorneys cannot properly provide such opinions without a keen understanding of the relevant obligations, nor are they able to execute relevant due diligence in case of, i.e., takeovers. They should genuinely try to discern the obligations in point. If they do not, they expose themselves and their clients to liability risks.[105]
- a focus on suppliers. As a rule, opting for suppliers that do not meet their obligations should require a justification;[106]
- a focus on supermarkets and other major retailers. In doing so, products such as meat could be scrutinised, i.e. by setting limits to the sale of huge quantities or at bottom prices;[107]
- more stringent impact assessments[108] of hugely GHG emitting activities, particularly for luxury and unnecessary products and services;[109]
- a ban on new permits for the exploration and production of oil and (shale) gas, unless there would be a very compelling justification for such activities, which is barely conceivable, except perhaps in the case of least developed or low-end developing countries.[110] In *Gloucester Resources v. Minister for Planning*, Judge Preston rightly

---

105 *See* in more detail Principle 48 of the updated EP and the commentary thereto p. 287/8.

106 *See* extensively the commentary to the updated EP p. 47 ff and Principle 18.

107 *See* the commentary to Principle 22 of the updated EP. For now a total ban of meat and meat products is probably a bridge too far. *See,* for a series of suggestions, in part very much in line with the EP, Emissions Gap Report 2020 chapter 6 (p. 62 ff).

108 *See* Principle 35 of the updated Principles and the commentary thereto p. 251 ff.

109 In *Wildearth Guardians et al. v. Bernhardt et al.*, the US District Court for the District of Columbia rules that "cumulative impacts' along with the direct and indirect impacts of a proposed action" need to be evaluated, i.e. "the incremental impact on the action when added to other past, present and reasonably foreseeable future actions regardless of what agency (Federal or non-Federal) or person undertakes such other actions". It can "result from individually minor but collectively significant actions taking place over a period of time", Civil Action No. 16-1724 (RC) of November 13, 2020 under IV A. In *Columbia Riverkeeper et al. v. US Army Corp of Engineers et al.*, the US District Court Western District of Washington at Tacoma, case no. 19-6071 RJB of 23 November 2020, http://climatecasechart.com/case/columbia-riverkeeper-v-us-army-corps-of-engineers/, held that all relevant factors must be considered: "among those are conservation, economics, aesthetics, general environmental concerns, wetlands, historic proprieties, fish and wildlife values, […] land use, […] shore erosion, recreation, […] and the needs of welfare to the people", under II D.

110 For a similar view without any exception Safe Climate, *id.* p. 36 under 78 (a); the Principles for Paris-Aligned Financial Institutions, www.ran.org/wp-content/uploads/2020/09/RAN_Principles_for_Paris-Aligned_Financial_Institutions.pdf, and Urgewalt et al., Five Years Lost Report, https://urgewald.org/five-years-lost, New Zealand bans new permits for offshore oil and gas exploration; *see* www.ecowatch.com/new-zealand-ends-new-offshore-oil-and-gas-drilling-2618531034.html and https://theticker.org/ticker/2019/12/9/new-zealand-to-ban-new-oil-and-gas-mining-by-2050-for-a-green-economy. Denmark bans new exploration and ends its oil and gas production from the North Sea by 2050; *see* www.spglobal.com/platts/en/market-insights/latest-news/natural-gas/120420-denmark-to-end-all-north-sea-oil-gas-production-by-2050-bans-new-exploration. *See* about other countries www.offshore-technology.com/features/countries-ending-oil-exploration/; on his first day in office President Biden issued a partial moratorium, https://

observed: "No new fossil fuel development is consistent with meeting the Paris accord climate targets."[111]

The view that there is, or at least should not be, room for the exploration of new oil and gas fields seems also to be taken by the US Court of Appeals for the Ninth Circuit in Ctr. For Bio. Diversity v. Zinke.[112] The Court was not saying and was not asked to say[113] that such explorations should be a no go, but it emphasised that the climate impact must be given genuine weight, the need to consider a "no action alternative"[114] and the "direct and indirect effects of the proposed action".[115]

Prospective plaintiffs should, however, realise that there is no guarantee to success, as the Norwegian case discussed under 5.4 illustrates. A recent case decided by the English Court of Appeal[116] also emphasises that the right case before the right' court matters. The case is about a development consent to approve a proposal to construct and operate two gas-fired generating units. These units would incorporate parts of two coal-fired units due to be decommissioned in 2022.[117] The judgment relies on the interpretation of the relevant English provisions, which implies that 'substantial weight' is to be given to 'considerations of need'. The decision maker has 'ample discretion to decide how best to go about making the evaluative judgment required".[118] "[I]n decision-making it is unnecessary 'to assess individual applications in terms of carbon emissions against carbon budgets'".[119] That does not mean that

> CO_2 emissions are irrelevant to a development consent, or cannot be given due weight in such a decision. It is simply that CO_2 emissions are not, of themselves, an automatic and insuperable obstacle to consent being given for any of the infrastructures for which EN-1 [the Overarching National Policy Statement for Energy] identifies a need and establishes a presumption in favour of approval.

---

insideclimatenews.org/news/21012021/biden-cancels-keystone-xl-and-halts-arctic-drilling-fossil-fuels/?utm_source=InsideClimate+News&utm_campaign=4de3412f4e-&utm_medium=email&utm_term=0_29c928ffb5-4de3412f4e-327952769.

111 Gloucester Resources v. Minister for Planning, (2019) NSWLEC 7 at 446 ff.
112 https://cdn.ca9.uscourts.gov/datastore/opinions/2020/12/07/18-73400.pdf.
113 See for the standard of review the judgment under IB (p. 10).
114 P. 12 with elaboration on the subsequent pages.
115 P. 16. See also David R. Boyd, Safe Climate: A Report of the Special Rapporteur on Human Rights and the Environment | UNEP, www.unep.org/resources/report/safe-climate-report-special-rapporteur-human-rights-and-environment p. 36 and the commentary to the EP p. 216.
116 ClientEarth v. Sec of State Business, [2021] EWCA Civ 43 (by Sir Keith Lindblom, the others agreeing).
117 See under 1 and 3.
118 Under 66 and 67.
119 Under 86.

It is for the decision maker to resolve how much weight is given to GHG emissions.[120]

Governments keen to grant permission or permit for new fossil fuel operations would be well advised to add a condition that the applicant fully accepts that the permission or permit can be terminated any time the government feels a need to do so for the purpose of reducing the country's GHG emissions as it thinks fit at the time of termination, whereas the applicant fully and unconditionally agrees that it can and will not seek any compensation in case of termination. Adding a clause along these lines may, and hopefully will, protect the government (in reality the taxpayer) against claims based on i.e. (de facto) expropriation and/or a violation of an investment treaty. It aims to emphasise that the entity seeking the permission realises and accepts that the prospective investment may 'strand' any time. That would be a double catch. First, it will bring applicants to understand the financial risk of new fossil operations, and it will avoid potentially heavy financial burdens on society if the operation needs to be phased earlier than expected. NGOs might consider seeking relief to the effect that such a clause is added to any permission or permit.

- a focus on the obligations of investors. A recent settlement between McVeigh and his pension fund Retail Employees Superannuation (Rest) illustrates the importance of this approach. According to a press release, Rest agrees

  that climate change is a material, direct and current financial risk to the superannuation fund' and 'that Rest [...] considers that it is important to actively identify and manage these issues.

Rest "will align its portfolio to net zero by 2050 and report against the Task Force on Climate-related Financial Disclosures".[121]

Investors could and should inter alia use their leverage to pressurise their investees to meet their obligations in the face of climate change.[122] That requires knowledge of these obligations. It is probably telling that investors do not show any interest even in discussions about such obligations.[123] Like most others, such as international organisations, central banks, auditors and enterprises, they are obsessed with disclosure. Disclosure is certainly a meaningful feature: it enables comparison of the performance or pledges of enterprises. But it does not shed any light on whether they legally suffice.

---

120 Under 87 with elaboration under 88-96.
121 Rest Reaches Settlement with Mark McVeigh, https://rest.com.au/why-rest/about-rest/news/rest-reaches-settlement-with-mark-mcveigh.
122 *See* in considerably more detail the commentary to the first edition of the EP p. 198 ff and Principles 36-44 of the updated EP and the commentary thereto.
123 *See*, also for references, the hurrah-message of Frank Bold, Countdown for the Reform that Will Overhaul Companies' Sustainability Reporting Obligations in Europe, www.allianceforcorporatetransparency.org/news/countdown-reform.html.

Academics would do the world a favour to research and analyse:
- the legal significance of pledges.[124]

In the context of its Heathrow judgment, the UK SC discussed the somewhat related issue of 'Government policy' at some length. It adopts "a relatively narrow meaning so that the relevant policies can readily be identified. Otherwise, civil servants would have to trawl through Hansard and press statements to see if anything had been said by a minister that might be characterised as 'policy'".[125] A similar approach might be adopted in the context of pledges. There are, however, many pledges that cannot easily be set aside as obscure;
- the legal status of codes of governance, conduct and other soft law instruments;[126]
- the role of climate science in shaping the law. More specifically, should the prevailing view of what needs to be done be the minimum basis for shaping legal obligations?[127]
- the role of the precautionary principle, which was revitalised in the Urgenda judgment. It clearly plays and should play a role in impact assessments. Its role in shaping reduction obligations is little self-explanatory because, *at any rate,* a hell of a lot needs to be done.[128] Introducing overly stringent obligations may (and probably will) mean that they will be ignored (the best is the enemy of the good);
- the climate scenario to be adopted and the weight *possible* future technical solutions should carry when determining reduction and other obligations;[129]
- tort law as (possible) legal basis for litigation;[130]

---

124 The number of pledges, both from (local) governments and business, is swiftly increasing; *see* Data-Driven EnviroLab & New Climate Institute, Accelerating Net Zero, https://newclimate.org/wp-content/uploads/2020/09/NewClimate_Accelerating_Net_Zero_Sept2020.pdf and the commentary to the updated EP p. 102 ff. Five Years Lost, How Finance is Blowing the Paris Carbon Budget, apparently supported by a series of NGOs, paints a gloomy picture of banks and investors financing fossil fuel companies. It contends that "the increasing number of pledges made by companies in the financial and energy sector to 'align with the Paris Agreement' or with 'net zero by 2050' can not be taken as anything other than greenwashing without meaningful immediate action to stop supporting fossil fuel expansion […]" (p. 73). These kinds of pledges may backfire.

125 *Id.* under 105. To me, the SC's view that the quotations under 72 do not suffice is quite understandable.

126 *See* the commentary to the updated EP p. 99 ff. Brunnée, Goldberg, Lord and Rajamani are right that "[l]awyers underestimate the importance of 'soft law' […]. As a result, they may miss the enormous potential effect, in political, reputational and other terms", in Richard Lord et al., Climate Change Liability Transnational Law and Practice p. 42; *see* about Mexico p. 645, Poland p. 440, Russia p. 518/9, South Africa p. 345 and the UK p. 482/3.

127 The IBA Model Statute for Proceedings Challenging Government Failure to Act on Climate Change Article 6.2 set limits to challenging IPCC reports. I do agree that, as a rule, they should be accepted as a minimum. Because the IPCC tends to lag behind the facts, owing to its impressive and time-consuming working method, there should be room for acceptance of more recent insights. In addition, the IPCC reports should be read carefully, particularly in regard to issues that they do *not* explicitly take into account.

128 *See* the commentary to the updated EP p. 95 ff.

129 *See* the commentary to the updated EP pp. 148 and 149.

130 *See* the commentary to the updated EP p. 91 ff.

- how to operationalise the minimum obligations feature, adopted by the Dutch Supreme Court in the Urgenda case,[131] by the Verwaltungsgericht Berlin[132] and in a draft document of the Committee on Legal Affairs of the European Parliament.[133] The feature is based on the idea that there are limits to what courts can do but that they at least have room to manoeuvre if a state, and others, I think, do not comply with the minimum they are legally required to do.

The fruit of this research and the features just mentioned were to be tested (further) in court, preferably in cases that stand a favourable chance.

7   THE 2050 PARADIGM

The '2050 paradigm' is capturing the minds of politicians, academics, investors, forerunners in the corporate world and NGOs. Courts also jumped on the bandwagon.[134] They seem to believe, or want to believe, that we have until 2050 to reduce global emissions to (net) zero. More likely than not, this is wishful thinking.[135]

This paradigm presupposes the availability of major carbon capture and storage or other techniques to 'offset' emissions on a relevant scale. Let us hope that they will be(come) available soon. For now, they are not available on a (sufficiently) large scale. If available, carbon storage will probably require long-lasting and expensive monitoring.[136] It is up to debate whether these techniques will be cheaper than a swift transition to renewable energy. Last, but certainly not least, those betting on 2050 seem to expect that all (or most) countries and enterprises are going to reduce their emissions to the extent necessary and at a great pace.[137] Much more likely than not, this is a phantom.

---

131 *See* the SC judgment in the Urgenda case under 6.2 and 6.3.

132 *Id.* pp. 22 and 23.

133 2020/2129(INL); *see* in particular Art. 1 para 2. *See also* my case note on Urgenda, NILR, *id.* p. 328 ff and 340 and 341.

134 *See* my case note under Urgenda, NILR 2020 pp. 331-334 and the French Tribunal administratif de Paris, *id.* under 16.

135 *See* extensively the commentary to the updated EP p. 28 ff. There are a few hopeful signals. Coal plays a less prominent role in the US electricity supply, in part because of the corona crisis, the lower demand and the low prices. It is in the laps of the gods whether this trend will reverse; *see* Brad Plumer, In a First, Renewable Energy is Poised to Eclipse Coal in the U.S., The New York Times 13 May 2020, www.nytimes.com/2020/05/13/climate/coronavirus-coal-electricity-renewables.html.

136 *See*, extensively, Michael G. Faure and Roy A. Partain, Carbon capture and storage, in particular pp. 24 ff, 107 ff, and 207; *see* for their balanced concluding observations (pp. 216 and 217).

137 China pledged to reduce its GHG emissions to net zero by 2060; China's Pledge to Be Carbon Neutral by 2060: What It Means, The New York Times (www.nytimes.com/2020/09/23/world/asia/china-climate-change.html). Compared with most other countries that is ambitious, but still after 2050. Unlike many other countries, China tends to achieve its pledges, if not realise them earlier than 'promised'.

This is not to say that it is necessarily mistaken to adopt the concept of net-zero emissions by 2050. An important reason for doing so could be pragmatism: being overly demanding or ambitious – i.e. requiring net-zero emissions by 2040 – entails the risk that very little will happen. Those taking a pragmatic position should, however, ask themselves: am I after what is within reach (pragmatism) or after solving the global problem (ambition)? Which stance will be taken by courts: will future judgments be based on what must, or had to, be done, instead of the maximum 'acceptable'? Will judgments requiring (net) zero emissions before 2050 be enforceable? The enforceability issue is not unimportant for entities that may consider ignoring judgments: the Urgenda case has shown that even in a self-acclaimed decent country, strongly advocating the rule of law (to others), it cannot be taken for granted that a State will comply with a judgment, not even if it is based on a minimum obligation.[138]

If one would opt for pragmatism, that stance should be confined to issues where it is the only realistic option, predominantly concerning the primary reduction obligation of States and enterprises. In many other instances, it would be a wrong, if unnecessary, choice. I.e. in relation to impact assessments, seeing that the relevant activities will often run for decades to come. We cannot afford unnecessary new emissions for many years to come. This, I think, reinforces my submission that there should be no room for new permits for the exploration and production of fossil fuels.[139]

8   THE 1.5°C PARADIGM

A staggering number of declarations, speeches, pledges, and what have you emphasise the need to prevent global temperature from going past 1.5°C.[140] That stance is laudable because passing that threshold is fraught with serious risk.[141] The authors of the updated EP believe that it is unlikely that we can still keep global warming below 1.5°C.[142] It may be possible to return to 1.5°C once the threshold is passed, but by then, much of the damage will already have been done.

---

138   *See* in more detail my NILR-contribution, *id.* p. 328 ff.

139   *Id.* p. 337 ff.

140   *See* also, for references, the commentary to the updated EP pp. 29 ff, 102, ff and 141-143. Without much ado Christina Voigt jumps on this bandwagon: in Kahl/Weller, *id.* p. 3 ("the 2018 IPCC report […] tells in very clear terms what needs to be done […] to get down to net zero around 2050 in order to keep global warming close to 1.5".

141   The magnitude of the risk is unknown, largely because opinions diverge on when tipping points will be passed; *see*, in more detail, the IPCC, Special Report, Global Warming of 1.5°C, Download Report (www.ipcc.ch/sr15/download/).

142   *See* the commentary to the updated EP p. 141 ff. The IPCC 2021-report was issued after submission of this contribution.

This begs the question of whether the aforementioned outings could create legal obligations.[143] As a rule, I have little doubt that they do *matter* in colouring vague legal norms. Thus, also the Urgenda judgment. The SC takes the view that the State had to explain why it had changed (downgraded) its ambition to reduce GHG emissions. The State was unable to convincingly explain why it had changed its mind.[144]

Depending on the circumstances, the defendant's answer could be as follows: we have genuinely tried, but it was too much of a challenge. Even though information about the major challenges of not passing the 1.5°C threshold is readily available, I do not have much doubt that this defence should be honoured if the allegation were true. In that scenario, a reasonable interpretation of the pledge would be that the relevant actor pledged truly bold action.[145] If courts would accept this interpretation, states and enterprises may regret this kind of laudable message.

9 The Looming Prospect of 2025 or 2030: The Unavoidability of Making Very Difficult Choices

Realistically speaking, the next five or ten years will largely be wasted in many countries and by many enterprises (not to speak of the public).[146] Should this happen, humankind, nature, the global economy, politicians and courts are in serious trouble. Politicians and courts will be confronted with increasingly inconvenient questions.[147] Because they cannot square the circle, *any* solution will be unsatisfactory to those whose interests are given less weight than those of others or, more bluntly, are sacrificed. The case about the climate refugee of Kiribati, mentioned under 5.5, is a perfect example. In the near future, the 'easy escape' will no longer be available.

In the most realistic scenario, by 2025 or 2030, only draconian measures will suffice to keep global warming well below 2°C. By then, a devil's dilemma will have been created for judges who would, in principle, be prepared to grant victory to plaintiffs seeking, i.e.,

---

143 An issue of wider importance because many enterprises do not comply with their 'pledges'; *see* Center for Political Accountability, Bloomberg Green, U.S. Businesses Say One Thing on Climate Change, But Their Campaign Giving Says Another, http://docplayer.net/196897214-Bloomberg-green-u-s-businesses-say-one-thing-on-climate-change-but-their-campaign-giving-says-another.html.

144 *See* my NILR contribution, *id.* p. 327. *See* for the more cautious position of the UK Supreme Court above under 5.6.

145 Commentary to the updated EP p. 104.

146 By way of example, AIM (European Brand Association) issued a statement on the EU Mandatory Human Rights Due Diligence (October 2020), www.aim.be/wp-content/themes/aim/pdfs/AIM%20Contribution%20to%20EU%20HRDD%20debate%20Oct%202020%20final.pdf?_t=1602836099. To quite some extent it is a useful contribution to the debate. The document emphasises the need to demonstrate that "they are taking reasonable steps", likely a sophistication for saying: we will do what we believe to be doable.

147 *See* about the role of courts M. Payandeh, in Kahl/Weller, *id.* p. 70 ff.

injunctive or declaratory relief to achieve far-reaching reductions within one or very few years (either or not including the non-achieved, but legally required, reductions between, say, 2020 and 2025).[148] They will have a choice between shaping obligations based on what is *reasonably doable* and what is *bitterly needed* or somewhere in between. They cannot appease their conscience by saying or thinking: you cannot expect me to *consider* judgments that will have a far-reaching negative impact on present-day society. As with all of us, they have a responsibility to avert catastrophe.

Over the centuries, it has been possible to shape the law to keep pace with the changing *demands* of society. In the context discussed here, the trick lies in the 'demands'. They will hugely diverge, depending on whose interests a court will focus on. It can only be hoped that judges will resist bending

> in the direction of the prevailing political wind. The criticisms of the elites and their ideas do not stop at the doors of the courthouse. Judges are subject to the slings and arrows of outraged governments, media and citizenry. It takes courage to act in the face of fire, to make unpopular decisions that will result in public denunciation of the decision and the decision-maker.[149]

I am not suggesting that all interests of the current generation, which includes newly born children, have to be sacrificed to 'the benefit' of the next generations, the environment and/or other living species. Rather, I am saying that we must start *thinking* about how to strike the 'best' compromise between the hugely diverging inter- and intragenerational interests and what would or should be the *upper limit* the law can offer to come to grips with climate change without serious backlashes.

What are the choices that *could* be made?

1. requiring extremely steep reduction curves. That implies (significantly) lower living standards in developed countries until the very moment that the economy can run on renewable energy, a situation that cannot materialise overnight. That does not necessarily mean that life will be less enjoyable. It may 'only' mean that we have to relinquish (part of) the often unnecessary luxury we are used to, in which scenario newly built runways, airports and the like may become stranded assets.[150] Make no mistake: this is not an unrealistic scenario.

---

148 If the earlier non-achieved reductions would be added, they have to be determined. The EP and the update contain submissions on how to calculate what was necessary. The OP, as amended in Principle 2.2.1 EP, offer a solution for calculating the primary reduction obligation of States; *see* for the temporal effect the commentary to the update p. 127 ff.

149 Brian J. Preston, The End of Enlightened Environmental Law?, *id.* p. 408.

150 *See* i.e. Lucy Colback, *id.*

More likely than not, developing countries cannot be spared unless wealthier countries are prepared to foot the bill of the measures they have to take. It is against the odds to assume that the developed countries are prepared to do so. It is obviously unfair to expect much from developing countries, but at the end of the day, it is also in their self-interest because climate change is a global problem. If climate change passes fatal thresholds, many vulnerable countries will be hit hardest. This creates a major challenge that ought to be solved in the international political arena. If, however, international politics fail in doing so (a not unlikely scenario), judges will have to answer these questions as best as they can.

2. to accept that global warming will increase by more than 2°C. That is a tricky choice because what will happen in that scenario is in the laps of the gods, seeing that dangerous tipping points will likely be passed. This much is clear: it will create a lot of hardship around the globe.

    If, i.e., injunctive relief is sought to reduce emissions by X%, a court could grant relief for 0.75x X%. To that effect, the concept of minimum obligations – i.e., the maximum the law can[151] offer without overstretching it – might be a legal panacea.[152]

3. to bet on technology or the use of insufficiently understood techniques such as geo-engineering.[153] This choice should not easily be adopted. After all, the price will be very high if it turns out that it was based on a miscalculation.

With a proviso mentioned at the bottom of this paragraph, the better – by no means ideal – choice is between options 1 and 2; it is by no means a self-explanatory choice. Each choice entails advantages for the current generation and, by the same token, disadvantages for nature and future generations, or the other way around. In-depth discussions will not result in the panacea. There is none. But such discussions will offer courts a basis for shaping their future judgments.

Do not blame me for not offering a clear choice between the devil and the deep blue sea. I am but the messenger, not the problem. The Oregon Chief Justice Walters is perfectly right in stating that

---

151 As explained before, that is a matter of judicial policy. Judges tend to be very effective to cast such a judgment in convincing language. Common law judges tend to be more open about policy arguments compared with continental European courts (our English friends may believe that 'continental European' is a pleonasm).

152 *See* the commentary to the update p. 84 ff and my NILR case note, *id.* pp. 328 ff, 340 and 341.

153 *See* – not about geoengineering – Michael B. Gerrard, Direct Air Capture: An Emerging Necessity to Fight Climate Change, https://climate.law.columbia.edu/sites/default/files/content/docs/Michael%20Gerrard/TR%20MarApr%202020%20Gerrard%20article.pdf. In his view, negative emissions are unavoidable because "even the most aggressive *plausible* reductions in emissions [...] would not keep us under 2.0C" (emphasis added). If the options mentioned under 1and 2 do not work or are rejected, Gerrard is probably right.

[t]he complexity of an issue may make a judicial decision more difficult, but it does not permit this court to abdicate its role.[154]

At the end of the day (hopefully not of humanity), courts will decide the role the law will play. It can only be hoped that most judges will feel the urgency to be relevant, which does not equate left-wing or, as some obstructionists may perceive it, 'socialist'. Relevancy in the realm of climate change is and should be unrelated to the divide between the political left and right. It is about the future of our planet. To paraphrase Gordon Brown: judges cannot avoid reconcile being radical and credible. If they do not, they will not achieve anything truly worthwhile.[155] Payandeh is right in stating that

courts will also have to take into account what is possible within a specific political climate [...]
[...] litigation [...] takes place with a societal space with media attention and public opinion as relevant factors[156] and
Even judges will not remain unimpressed by the prevailing opinions in society and science and might be more willing to advance progressive climate protection goals when society at large feels the pressing need for action.[157]

Realistically speaking, however, it is against the odds to expect that courts will opt for 1. Such a choice will be decried as a *gouvernement des juges*. If that ever becomes a reality, it is doomed to be short-lived.

Seeing the precautionary principle and the vital interests of vulnerable countries, people and the environment, a sound legal basis would exist for far-reaching measures to be taken right now, if sought by means of, i.e., injunctive relief. Seeing the fate of significantly less ambitious claims it belabours the obvious that there are boundaries to what courts are *prepared* to do. However regrettable, one cannot blame courts for being unprepared to render truly revolutionary judgments that do not stand any chance of acceptance. In our wicked world, judges cannot square the circle. Let us hope that many will go to the very outer limits of 'the acceptable', an unavoidably ambiguous concept.

Although unlikely, in the years to come, public opinion may change. In the course of just a few years, a not unimportant part of public opinion has radicalised 'thanks' to some powerful news outlets and polarising politicians. At the same time, we have experienced a growing sense of urgency, fuelled in part by organisations such as extinction-rebellion.

---

154 *Chernaik v. Brown*, 367 Or 143 (2020) at 186.
155 Gordon Brown, My Life, Our Time p. 437.
156 *Id.* p. 75.
157 Payandeh, *id.* p. 76.

Although unlikely, it is not inconceivable that in the near future truly courageous judgments will be widely applauded, which would be a double catch. They will feel more comfortable stretching the law to cope with the urgent need for very swift and bold action, and it will limit the risk of politicisation of their judgments.

As things stand now, it would be overly demanding to expect that judges assume full responsibility for the failure of society to reduce global GHG emissions to the extent required. Such a stance would be as convincing as the claims initiated by a few lower branches of the US government suing, for practical purposes, 'big oil' for putting fossil fuels on the market they did and do need because they made themselves dependent on such products.

10   WORST-CASE SCENARIOS MANAGEABLE?

A 2015 report by The Economist Intelligence Unit seems to suggest that the financial consequences of a rise of global temperature by 6°C is bearable for investors.[158] The discounted adverse impact on the value of their assets would be 'only' 10% of the global total.[159]

This figure seems unrealistically low. Assuming that the calculations make any sense, which would be quite a miracle in light of a great many uncertainties about what will happen in such a scenario, it is certainly no reason for leaning backwards. A rise of global temperature by 6°C – and even significantly less – will have cataclysmic consequences for nature and billions of people: illnesses, extreme poverty and the need to move to other places where few of them will be welcomed, to mention just a few. In financial terms, these evils *may* be limited; it would be hugely irresponsible to focus on investors' losses or the economic angle only. If that would be what the law has to offer, lawyers should hang their harp on the willows.

11   SUPPORTING POTENTIALLY USEFUL SUGGESTIONS

Climate change is a breeding ground for an unheard-of number of initiatives, strategies and new legal features. Those behind these initiatives often believe that their hobby horse is the panacea to come to grips with climate change. When I started working on climate change approximately 20 years ago, I also believed that my ideas would solve 'all' problems. I was naïve. Over time I came to understand that climate change is such a daunting and

---

158   Since 2015 a lot has happened. That means that the figures are outdated, but they are still illustrative.
159   https://eiuperspectives.economist.com/sustainability/cost-inaction/white-paper/cost-inaction.

terribly complex problem that there is no single solution. Every idea, strategy or initiative that can contribute, however small, counts. Only with the benefit of hindsight, we will be able to judge which contributions were most effective.

All those who are genuinely willing to contribute to solutions – many more people and organisations than one might think of – deserve our respect and support. I am not saying that we should unconditionally support ideas that, in our eyes and in spite of their merits, may entail more disadvantages than advantages. However, when discussing the potentially adverse consequences of ideas submitted by others, we should keep an eye out for the positive effects they could generate.

As to liability for climate change losses, for many years, I have been a crusader against such liability. I still believe that crushing liability is more of an evil than leaving many victims uncompensated. I do, however, understand that the prospect of potential liability *may* have a deterrent effect, although I am not a believer in that effect. In addition, to the extent reasonably possible, we should lend our ears to bearable liability with a focus on poor people, vulnerable countries and nature.[160]

In the context of climate change, the concept of obligations towards Mother Earth, or the flip side obligations towards nature, is too vague to be operable, I think. To the extent these features could serve as a game changer for courts, politicians or the boards of enterprises, they entail a significant value.[161] In that scenario, observations along the lines

---

160 *See* footnote 35.

161 They may also contribute to a shift of paradigm in the legal arena. In the realm of (traditional) liability law the right to life, bodily and mental integrity, human dignity and liberty 'enjoy' the most extensive protection (Art. 2:102 para 2 PETL); with the benefit of hindsight (I was one of the drafters), it is surprising that 'nature' is not even mentioned. Art. 2:209 PEL Liab. Dam mentions "substantially impaired natural elements constituting the environment, such as air, water, soil, flora and fauna"; *see* for elaboration from a comparative angle Christian von Bar, Principles of European Law, Non-Contractual Liability Arising out of Damage Caused to Another p. 532 ff. *See* about rights of nature inter alios Alice Bleby, Rights of Nature as a Response to the Anthropocene, 48 Univ. West. Aust. Law Rev. 33 (2020), Laura Burgers, Justitia, the People's Power and Mother Earth, in particular p. 283 ff, A New Beginning for People and Nature, EU Green Week 2020 Conference – Flash Report and a letter of 14 September 2020 to members of the core group on human rights and the environment, R2E letter 4 (www.universal-rights.org/wp-content/uploads/2020/09/Letter-on-the-right-to-environment-150920-generic.pdf); over a thousand organisations called for the recognition of a human right of all to a safe, clean, healthy and sustainable environment: The Time is Now!, Humanium Joins Global Call for Right to a Healthy Environment, www.humanium.org/en/humanium-joins-global-call-for-right-to-a-healthy-environment/; they point to a "substantial majority of States [that] have already incorporated a right to a healthy environment in their Constitutions and laws" (p. 2). A statement of the New York City Bar (NYCB), Support for the Formal Recognition by the United Nations of the Human Right to a Healthy Environment, https://s3.amazonaws.com/documents.nycbar.org/files/2020751-HumanRighttoHealthyEnvironment.pdf; the NYCB does acknowledge that "[m]ore is needed, on a the local, national and international level" and that "the recognition of such a right is no panacea" (p. 6). I doubt whether it will "lead to improved implementation of environmental laws and regulations, and better enforcement" (p. 7), although it *could* and hopefully will. *See also* Klaus Bosselman's inspiring Earth Governance, Trusteeship of the Global commons. I agree with his analysis that states and the international community fall short. "[M]ore [State] sovereignty where possible, less sovereignty where necessary" (p. 269)

"we do not need them because they do not add anything to what the law already offers" are not overly helpful. In 'ordinary' cases, such rights, though rather undetermined, could indeed "play a crucial role for the realization of environmental justice for communities exposed to degraded, hazardous and threatening environments".[162] Because almost all human activities compromise nature, it is useful, if not necessary, to determine what these rights mean in terms of the obligations of concrete players. Few people will challenge the importance of a clean and healthy environment, but a concretisation of the debate would be helpful to achieve that goal.

I realise – and know from many years of experience – that it is not easy to strike the right balance between support and constructive criticism. This leaves my key point untouched: to the extent possible, "let a hundred flowers bloom" is the best strategy. "The advancements that bend the arc of history come from steps that are never taken alone."[163]

12   FINALLY

This much is clear: the future will be different. It is still possible to stem the tide.[164] Even if tipping points are passed, even if climate change cannot be kept (well) below 2°C or, God forbid, below 3°C, there will be a future, albeit not the future we want. The sun will set again, but the dawn will be different. How different depends on us.

> [H]ortatory statements of principles and aspirational goals are insufficient: the grand strategy must be translated into action.[165]

The good news is Eva Schulev's new institute. No doubt she, her colleagues, friends and staff will contribute to stemming the tide. That is a Herculean task. We can only congratulate her and the University of Graz on this brilliant initiative. May the Institute flourish. It would be a blessing to the world.

---

may help to overcome the deadlocked positions, but much will depend on the concretisation and implementation of this idea. It may well be a contribution to a global solution and, in an ideal world, the panacea.

162 The Time is Now!, *id.* p. 3.

163 Gordon Brown, *id.* p. 460.

164 After finalising this contribution, glimmers of hope appeared on the horizon; *see* Bob Berwyn, Many Scientists Now Say Global Warming Could Stop Relatively Quickly After Emissions Go to Zero, https://inside climate-news.org/news/03012021/five-aspects-climate-change-2020/?utm_source=InsideClimate+News&utm_campaign=4946d527ef-&utm_medium=email&utm_term=0_29c928ffb5-4946d527ef-327952769.

165 Brian J. Preston, The Judicial Development of the Precautionary Principle, 35 EPLJ 141 (2018).

Bibliography

Benjamin, We, the Judges, and the Environment, 29 Pace Environmental Law Review 2012, 582.

Berwyn, Many Scientists Now Say Global Warming Could Stop Relatively Quickly After Emissions Go to Zero, https://insideclimatenews.org/news/03012021/five-aspects-climate-change-2020/?utm_source=InsideClimate+News&utm_campaign=4946d527ef-&utm_medium=email&utm_term=0_29c928ffb5-4946d527ef-327952769.

Bhullar, The Polluter Pays Principle: Scope and Limits of Court Decisions, in *Ghosh* (ed.), Indian Environmental Law, Key Concepts and Principles (2019).

Bleby, Rights of Nature as a Response to the Anthropocene, 48 University of Western Australia Law Review 2020, 33.

Boer, The University of Sydney Law School Legal Studies Research Paper Series, No. 20/25, April 2020, The Preamble, http://www.austlii.edu.au/au/journals/USydLRS/2020/13.pdf.

Bold, Countdown for the Reform that Will Overhaul Companies' Sustainability Reporting Obligations in Europe, www.allianceforcorporatetransparency.org/news/countdown-reform.html.

Bradshaw/Ehrlich et al., Underestimating the Challenges of Avoiding a Ghastly Future, www.frontiersin.org/articles/10.3389/fcosc.2020.615419/full.

Brown, My Life, Our Times (2018).

Burgers, Justitia, the People's Power and Mother Earth, Democratic Legitimacy of Judicial Law-making in European Private Law Cases on Climate Change (2020).

Business & Human Rights Resource Centre, Support for EU Framework on Mandatory Human Rights and Environmental Due Diligence, www.business-humanrights.org/en/latest-news/support-for-eu-framework-on-mandatory-human-rights-and-environmental-due-diligence/.

Carnwath, Human Rights and the Environment, www.supremecourt.uk/docs/speech-190620.pdf.

CDP, Foundations for Science-Based Net-Zero Target Setting in the Corporate Sector, https://sciencebasedtargets.org/resources/legacy/2020/09/foundations-for-net-zero-full-paper.pdf (September 2020).

Center for Political Accountability, Bloomberg Green: U.S. Businesses Say One Thing on Climate Change, But Their Campaign Giving Says Another, Microsoft Word - CPA - Bloomberg Green - U.S. Businesses Say One Thing on Climate Change, But Their Campaign Giving Says Another - 10-23-20 - CPA quoted.docx (politicalaccountability.net).

Chow, New Zealand Ends New Offshore Oil and Gas Exploration, www.ecowatch.com/new-zealand-ends-new-offshore-oil-and-gas-drilling-2618531034.html.

CIEL, Groundbreaking Inquiry in Philippines Links Carbon Majors to Human Rights Impacts of Climate Change, Calls for Greater Accountability, www.ciel.org/news/groundbreaking-inquiry-in-philippines-links-carbon-majors-to-human-rights-impacts-of-climate-change-calls-for-greater-accountability/.

Colback, The Role of Business in Climate Change, www.ft.com/content/7ab0bfb0-b37c-463d-b132-0944b6fe8e8b.

Commodity Futures Trading Commission, CFTC's Climate-Related Market Risk Subcommittee Releases Report, www.cftc.gov/PressRoom/PressReleases/8234-20.

Data-Driven EnviroLab/New Climate Institute, Accelerating Net Zero, Exploring Cities, Regions and Companies' Pledges to Decarbonise, https://newclimate.org/wp-content/uploads/2020/09/NewClimate_Accelerating_Net_Zero_Sept2020.pdf.

European Brands Association, EU Mandatory Human Rights Due Diligence, www.aim.be/wp-content/themes/aim/pdfs/AIM%20Contribution%20to%20EU%20HRDD%20debate%20Oct%202020%20final.pdf?_t=1602836099.

European Commission, EU Green Week Puts the Spotlight on Nature as Our Strongest Ally in Green Recovery, https://ec.europa.eu/environment/news/eu-green-week-puts-spotlight-nature-our-strongest-ally-green-recovery-2020-10-16_en.

European Parliament Committee on Legal Affairs 11 September 2020, Draft Report, 2020/2129(INL).

European Parliament 17 December 2020, Resolution on Sustainable Corporate Governance, 2020/2137/INI).

Expert Group on Global Climate Change, Principles on Climate Obligations of Enterprises, also available at www.climateprinciplesforenterprises.org.

Fabius, Speech by Laurent Fabius, President of the French Constitutional Council, at the European Court of Human Rights, www.echr.coe.int/Documents/Speech_20190125_Fabius_JY_ENG.pdf.

Freshfields Bruckhaus Deringer, Business and Human Rights, www.freshfields.com/en-gb/our-thinking/campaigns/biz-human-rights/.

Gardner, The Cost of Inaction, https://eiuperspectives.economist.com/sustainability/cost-inaction/white-paper/cost-inaction.

Gerrard, Direct Air Capture: An Emerging Necessity to Fight Climate Change, https://climate.law.columbia.edu/sites/default/files/content/docs/Michael%20Gerrard/TR%20MarApr%202020%20Gerrard%20article.pdf (2020).

Gerrard, The Role of Lawyers in Decarbonizing Society, www.stanfordlawreview.org/online/the-role-of-lawyers-in-decarbonizing-society/.

GRI/University of Stellenbosch Business School, Carrots & Sticks Sustainability Reporting Policy: Global Trends in Disclosure as the ESG Agenda Goes Mainstream, www.usb.ac.za/wp-content/uploads/2020/08/Carrots-Sticks-2020-Report-FIN-21.07.2020.pdf (2020).

Hinteregger, Civil Liability and the Challenges of Climate Change: A Functional Analysis, JETL 2017, 238.

Hook, Oil Majors Gear Up for Wave of Climate Change Liability Lawsuits, www.ft.com/content/d5fbeae4-869c-11e9-97ea-05ac2431f453.

IHRB, Just Transitions for All – Business, Human Rights and Climate Action, www.ihrb.org/focus-areas/just-transitions/report-just-transitions-for-all.

IMF, World Economic Outlook, October 2020: A Long and Difficult Ascent, www.imf.org/en/Publications/WEO/Issues/2020/09/30/world-economic-outlook-october-2020.

International Bar Association, International Bar Association Climate Crisis Statement, https://www.ibanet.org/MediaHandler?id=822c1967-f851-4819-8200-2fe298164922.

IPCC, Climate Change 2007: Synthesis Report Summary for Policymakers, www.ipcc.ch/site/assets/uploads/2018/02/ar4_syr_spm.pdf.

IPCC, Special Report, Global Warming of 1.5°C, Download Report, www.ipcc.ch/sr15/download/.

Kahl/Weller (eds), Climate Change Litigation, Handbook (2021).

Kusnetz, Biden Cancels Keystone XL, Halts Drilling in Arctic Refuge on Day One, Signaling a Larger Shift Away From Fossil Fuels, https://insideclimatenews.org/news/21012021/biden-cancels-keystone-xl-and-halts-arctic-drilling-fossil-fuels/?utm_source=Inside Climate+News&utm_campaign=4de3412f4e-&utm_medium=email&utm_term=0_29c928ffb5-C4de3412f4e-327952769.

La Fayette, International Liability for Damage to the Environment, in *Fitzmaurice/Ong/Merkouris* (eds), Research Handbook on International Environmental Law (2010).

Letter to the Members of the core group on human rights and the environment, EU Green Week 2020 Conference, www.universal-rights.org/wp-content/uploads/2020/09/Letter-on-the-right-to-environment-150920-generic.pdf.

Liu/Ciais/Deng et al., Near-Real-Time Monitoring of Global CO2 Emissions Reveals the Effects of the COVID-19 Pandemic, https://rdcu.be/b9l1Z.

Lombrana/Warren, A Pandemic that Cleared Skies and that Halted Cities Isn't Slowing Global Warming, www.bloomberg.com/graphics/2020-how-coronavirus-impacts-climate-change/.

Lord/Goldberg/Rajamani/Brunnée (eds), Climate Change Liability Transnational Law and Practice (2011).

Moréteau, Le droit commun outil de gestion citoyenne des biens communs maritimes et terrestres (not yet published).

Myers, China's Pledge to Be Carbon Neutral by 2060: What It Means, www.nytimes.com/2020/09/23/world/asia/china-climate-change.html.

New Climate Institute, Climate Neutrality Claims, How to Distinguish Between Climate Leadership and Greenwashing, https://newclimate.org/2020/09/14/climate-neutrality-claims/.

New York City Bar, Statement of the New York City Bar Association, Support for the Formal Recognition by the United Nations of the Human Right to a Healthy Environment, https://s3.amazonaws.com/documents.nycbar.org/files/2020751-HumanRightto HealthyEnvironment.pdf.

OECD, OECD Due Diligence Guidance for Responsible Business Conduct, https://mneguidelines.oecd.org/OECD-Due-Diligence-Guidance-for-Responsible-Business-Conduct.pdf (2018).

OHCHR, Five UN Human Rights Treaty Bodies Issue a Joint Statement on Human Rights and Climate Change, www.ohchr.org/en/NewsEvents/Pages/DisplayNews.aspx?NewsID=24998&LangID=E.

OHCHR, United Nations Human Rights Treaty Body Database, https://tbinternet.ohchr.org/_layouts/15/treatybodyexternal/Download.aspx?symbolno=CCPR%2fC%2f127%2fD%2f2728%2f2016&Lang=en.

Okawa, Responsibility for Environmental Damage, in *Fitzmaurice/Ong/Merkouris* (eds), Research Handbook on International Environmental Law (2010).

Perkins, Denmark to End all North Sea Oil, Gas Production by 2050, Bans New Exploration, www.spglobal.com/platts/en/market-insights/latest-news/natural-gas/120420-denmark-to-end-all-north-sea-oil-gas-production-by-2050-bans-new-exploration.

Perry-Kessaris, Corporate Liability for Environmental Harm, in *Fitzmaurice/Ong/Merkouris* (eds), Research Handbook on International Environmental Law (2010).

Plumer, In a First, Renewable Energy is Poised to Eclipse Coal in the U.S., www.nytimes.com/2020/05/13/climate/coronavirus-coal-electricity-renewables.html.

Preston, Characteristics of Successful Environmental Courts and Tribunals, http://www2.law.mercer.edu/elaw/environmental%20courts.pdf.

Preston, The End of Enlightened Environmental Law, Journal of Environmental Law 2019, 399.

Preston, The Influence of the Paris Agreement on Litigation: Legal Obligations and Norms, Journal of Environmental Law 2021, 33.

Preston, The Judicial Development of the Precautionary Principle, Environmental Planning Law Journal 2018, 123.

Principles for Responsible Investment, Why and How Investors Should Act on Human Rights, www.unpri.org/human-rights-and-labour-standards/why-and-how-investors-should-act-on-human-rights/6636.article.

Raimondi, Opening speech by President Guido Raimondi at the European Court of Human Rights, www.echr.coe.int/Documents/Speech_20190125_Raimondi_JY_ENG.pdf.

Rainforest Action Network, Principles for Paris-Aligned Financial Institutions, Climate Impact, Fossil Fuels and Deforestation, www.ran.org/wp-content/uploads/2020/09/RAN_Principles_for_Paris-Aligned_Financial_Institutions.pdf.

Razzaque, Human rights to a clean environment: procedural rights, in *Fitzmaurice/Ong/Merkouris* (eds), Research Handbook on International Environmental Law (2010).

Rest, Rest Reaches Settlement with Mark McVeigh, https://rest.com.au/why-rest/about-rest/news/rest-reaches-settlement-with-mark-mcveigh.

Sachs, Amy Coney Barrett Showed She's Ready to be Part of Trump's Post-truth Strategy, www.jeffsachs.org/newspaper-articles/8x9btnsazlta5nfxw8bkbefbks23nc.

Schrijver, The Evolution of Sustainable Development in International Law: Inception, Meaning and Status (2009).

Shelton, Remedies in International Human Rights Law (3rd ed., 2015).

Spier, Injunctive Relief: Opportunities and Challenges: Thoughts About a Potentially Promising Vehicle to Stem the Tide, in *Spier/Magnus* (eds), Climate Change Remedies (2014).

Spier, Liability for Climate Change Losses: A Blessing or a Curse, in *Beekhoven van den Boezem/Jansen/Schuijling* (eds), Sustainability and Financial Markets (2019).

Spier, Mistake of Law and Sustainability, in *Karner/Magnus/Spier/Widmer* (eds), Essays in Honour of Helmut Koziol (2020).

Spier, Presentation of Prof. Dr. Jaap Spier, EU Green Week, https://climateprinciplesforenterprises.org/presentation-of-prof-dr-jaap-spier-eu-green-week/ (last accessed 22 October 2020).

Spier, Private Law as a Crowbar for Coming to Grips with Climate Change, KNVIR Preadviezen 2018.

Spier, Shaping Law for Global Crises: Thoughts about the Role the Law Could Play to Come to Grips with the Major Challenges of Our Time (2012).

Spier, Strategies to Keep Global Warming Below 2 Degrees to Avoid Devastating Liability, Prepared for the PRI in Person Conference, San Francisco 2018, https://custom.cvent.com/A7020F0F9A8247B2A6095E2EF0DC7D77/files/Event/5a2f15d64e534edb8f77813a1c7eb7de/cb1ae2a16cb54bb7a913403abf02e219.pdf.

Spier, The Rule of Law and Judicial Activism: Obstacles for Shaping the Law to Meet the Demands of a Civilized Society, Particularly in Relation to Climate Change? in *Faure/Van der Walt* (eds), Globalization and Private Law (2010).

Spier, The "Strongest" Climate Ruling Yet': The Dutch Supreme Court's Urgenda Judgement, Netherlands International Law Review 2020, 319.

Spitzer/Butscher, Liability for Climate Change: Cases, Challenges and Concepts, JETL 2017, 137.

Sustainable Markets Initiative, Terra Carta, For Nature, People & Planet, www.sustainable-markets.org/TerraCarta_Charter_Jan11th2021.pdf.

The Climate Docket, Carbon Majors Can Be Held Liable for Human Rights Violations, Philippines Commission Rules, www.climatedocket.com/2019/12/09/philippines-human-rights-climate-change-2/.

The Commonwealth, Commonwealth Declarations, https://thecommonwealth.org/sites/default/files/inline/Commonwealth_Declarations_070619.pdf.

The EUFJE Budapest 2014 Conference Declaration on Environmental Responsibility, www.eufje.org/images/docConf/bud2014/Declaration_environmental_responsibility.pdf.

The Portal for Sustainability Reporting, The Sustainability Board Report 2020, f6724f_9d0f1b6de2e346a7b0e4fdc163039a98.pdf.

Thum, Humanium Joins Global Call for Right to Healthy Environment, www.humanium.org/en/humanium-joins-global-call-for-right-to-a-healthy-environment/.

UK Government, United Kingdom of Great Britain and Northern Ireland's Nationally Determined Contribution, https://assets.publishing.service.gov.uk/government/uploads/system/uploads/attachment_data/file/943618/uk-2030-ndc.pdf (2020).

UN Environment Programme, Emissions Gap Report 2020, www.unep.org/emissions-gap-report-2020.

UN Environment Programme et al, The Production Gap, 2019 Report, www.unep.org/resources/report/production-gap-report-2019.

UN Human Rights Special Procedures, Safe Climate, A Report of the Special Rapporteur on Human Rights and the Environment, https://wedocs.unep.org/bitstream/handle/20.500.11822/30158/Safe_Climate_Report.pdf?sequence=1&isAllowed=y.

UNEP, Safe Climate: A Report of the Special Rapporteur on Human Rights and the Environment, www.unep.org/resources/report/safe-climate-report-special-rapporteur-human-rights-and-environment.

United Nations Climate Change, The Paris Agreement, https://unfccc.int/process-and-meetings/the-paris-agreement/the-paris-agreement.

United Nations Climate Change, What is the United Nations Framework Convention on Climate Change? https://unfccc.int/process-and-meetings/the-convention/what-is-the-united-nations-framework-convention-on-climate-change.

Urgewald Anwalt für Umwelt und Menschenrechte, Five Years Lost Report, How Finance Is Blowing the Paris Carbon Budget, https://urgewald.org/five-years-lost (2020).

Voigt/Makuch (eds), Courts and the Environment (2018).

Von Bar, Principles of European Law, Non-Contractual Liability Arising out of Damage Caused to Another (2009).

WHO, Climate Change and Health, www.who.int/news-room/fact-sheets/detail/climate-change-and-health.

Worland, Climate Change Could Cause More Annual Deaths than Infectious Disease by 2100, https://time.com/5876229/climate-change-death-rate/.

World Commission on Environmental Law, IUCN World Declaration on the Environmental Rule of Law, www.iucn.org/sites/dev/files/content/documents/english_world_declaration_on_the_environmental_rule_of_law_final.pdf.

Cases

Australia

Gloucester Resources v. Minister for Planning (2019) NSWLEC 7, http://climatecasechart.com/climate-change-litigation/non-us-case/gloucester-resources-limited-v-minister-for-planning/.

Canada

Dini Ze' v. Canada, 2020 FC 1059, http://climatecasechart.com/climate-change-litigation/non-us-case/gagnon-et-al-v-her-majesty-the-queen/.

Environnement Jeunesse v. Canada, http://climatecasechart.com/non-us-case/environnement-jeunesse-v-canadian-government/.

France

Conseil d'Etat 19 November 2020, *Grande-Synthe*, https://www.conseil-etat.fr/fr/arianeweb/CE/decision/2020-11-19/427301.

Tribunal administratif de Paris 3 February 2021, *Oxfam France v. France*, http://paris.tribunal-administratif.fr/content/download/179360/1759761/version/1/file/1904967190496819049721904976.pdf.

Germany

Verwaltungsgericht Berlin 31 October 2019, VG 10 K 412.18, https://openjur.de/u/2252318.html.

Ireland

Friends of the Irish Environment CLG v. and Fingal County Council, http://climatecasechart.com/non-us-case/friends-irish-environment-clg-v-fingal-county-council/.

New Zealand

Smith v. Fonterra Co-Operative Group Limited, NZHC 419, http://climatecasechart.com/climate-change-litigation/non-us-case/smith-v-fronterra-co-operative-group-limited/.

Norway

Borgarting Court of Appeal 23 January 2020, *The People v. Arctic Oil*, 18-060499ASD-BORG/03, https://cer.org.za/virtual-library/judgments/foreign-and-international-courts/the-people-v-arctic-oil-nature-and-youth-greenpeace-v-norways-ministry-of-petroleum-and-energy.

Supreme Court of Norway 22 December 2020, www.domstol.no/en/Enkelt-domstol/supremecourt/rulings/2020/supreme-court-civil-cases/hr-2020-2472-p/.

The Netherlands

Hoge Raad 20 December 2019, *Urgenda*, ECLI:NL:HR:2019:2007, https://uitspraken.rechtspraak.nl/inziendocument?id=ECLI:NL:HR:2019:2007.

District Court of The Hague 9 December 2020, ECLI:NL:RBDHA:2020:12440, https://uitspraken.rechtspraak.nl/inziendocument?id=ECLI:NL:RBDHA:2020:12440.

United Kingdom

ClientEarth v. Secretary of State for Business, Energy and Industrial Strategy and Drax Power Limited, C1/2020/0998/QBACF, https://www.judiciary.uk/wp-content/uploads/2021/01/ClientEarth-v-Sec.-of-State-for-business-energy-and-industrial-strategy-judment.pdf.

Friends of the Earth Ltd and others v. Heathrow Airport Ltd, [2020] UKSC 52, https://www.supremecourt.uk/cases/docs/uksc-2020-0042-judgment.pdf.

United States

American Lung Association et al v. Environmental Protection Agency, http://climatecasechart.com/climate-change-litigation/case/american-lung-association-v-epa/.

Bernhardt, Center for Biological Diversity et al v. Bureau of Ocean Energy Management, United States Fish and Wildlife Service, http://climatecasechart.com/climate-change-litigation/case/center-for-biological-diversity-v-zinke-3/.

Chernaik v. Brown, 367 Or 143 (Or. 2020), http://climatecasechart.com/climate-change-litigation/case/chernaik-v-kitzhaber/.

Columbia Riverkeepers v. US Army Corps of Engineers, http://climatecasechart.com/climate-change-litigation/case/columbia-riverkeeper-v-us-army-corps-of-engineers/.

Juliana v. United States, No. 18-36082, http://climatecasechart.com/climate-change-litigation/case/juliana-v-united-states/.

Wildearth Guardians et al v. Bernhardt et al, http://climatecasechart.com/climate-change-litigation/case/wildearth-guardians-v-bernhardt/.

CLIMATE LAW AND CLIMATE SCIENCE: JOINT ENABLER OF A NEW CLIMATE ENLIGHTENMENT?

Oliver C. Ruppel

1 INTRODUCTION

The following text is an updated version of my presentation held on the splendid occasion of the official opening of ClimLaw: The new Research Center for Climate Law at the University of Graz on 17 June 2020.[1] I structure my thoughts in several brief and interrelated (but by no means conclusive) parts, namely the climate crisis in the Anthropocene; climate law and litigation; the nexus between climate law and climate science; climate justice pathways for a new climate enlightenment; science informs law, law shapes behaviour; and some concluding remarks.

2 THE CLIMATE CRISIS IN THE ANTHROPOCENE

The 'diagnosis' of planet Earth seems rather clear in that constantly growing human and industrial activities have caused dramatically increased emissions of greenhouse gases, which in turn cause the global climate to change rapidly and probably irreversibly. The 'symptoms' of climate change are likely to cause more and more natural disasters, extreme weather events and climate-induced migration movements with the potential to cause national and cross-boundary conflict and thus endanger global peace and security. The 'therapy' against these symptoms is much less clear, and I would like to argue that more coherence between climate science and climate law will be required to cope with the challenges ahead.[2]

In an age shaped primarily by people, the Anthropocene, mankind is faced with enormous challenges posed by the effects of climate change, de facto and de jure. The

---

1   The official opening of ClimLaw: Graz, 17 June 2020, Online Conference.

2   Ruppel, OC (2013) Intersections of Law and Cooperative Global Climate Governance – Challenges in the Anthropocene. In: Ruppel, OC, Roschmann, C & K Ruppel-Schlichting (eds) *Climate Change: International Law and Global Governance Volume I: Legal Responses and Global Responsibility.* Baden-Baden, Nomos Law Publishers, 29-93, 30.

expansion of mankind, both in numbers and per capita exploitation of Earth's resources,[3] has been astounding and is fraught with severe consequences for present and future generations.[4]

A daunting task lies ahead during the era of the Anthropocene, which requires appropriate human behaviour at all scales. The climate crisis – like every global crisis – impacts the international system, its structures, norms and institutions. In light of the current COVID-19 crisis, there is no need to go back to the world wars and the founding of the League of Nations and the United Nations in order to support this statement.[5]

3   CLIMATE LAW AND LITIGATION

As we all know, the law is the major instrument by which mature societies consolidate their internal and external relationships. And without legal rules, the life of a society becomes unpredictable and aleatory.[6] Subsuming climate change under any such legal structure is a challenging task owing to the endless ramifications of climate change and particularly because of its complexity, interdisciplinary nature and impacts on various – if not all – segments of our planet and society. This is why climate change can – if at all – be tackled only through a combination of political but particularly legal and natural science tools.

When climate change is viewed from a legal perspective, it has, of course, given rise to the evolution of various principles and concepts of international law, including the notion of common concern of humankind and the need for protection of the most vulnerable.[7] Climate law is both international and domestic in nature and includes complementary dimensions, procedural and substantive.[8]

---

3   *Cf.* Ruppel, OC (2012) Wasser und Land – Brennpunkte innerhalb der Entwicklungsgemeinschaft des südlichen Afrikas (SADC). In: Reder, M & H Pfeifer (eds) *Kampf um Ressourcen. Weltordnung zwischen Konkurrenz und Kooperation – Globale Solidarität, Schritte zu einer neuen Weltkultur.* Band 22. Stuttgart, Kohlhammer Verlag, 59-85.

4   Ruppel (2013) 30.

5   *See* Perthes, V (2020) The Corona Crisis and International Relations: Open Questions, Tentative Assumptions. *Stiftung Wissenschaft und Politik Point of View* at www.swp-berlin.org/en/publication/the-corona-crisis-and-international-relations-open-questions-tentative-assumptions/, last accessed 25 February 2021.

6   Tomuschat, C (2012) Risk and Security in International Law. In: Hestermeyer, HP, König, D, Matz-Lück, N, Röben, V, Seibert-Fohr, A, Stoll, PT & S Vöneki (eds) *Coexistence, Cooperation and Solidarity: Liber Amicorum Rüdiger Wolfrum.* Leiden, Martinus Nijhoff Publishers, 1283-1308, 1283.

7   Schrijver, N (2011) The Impact of Climate Change: Challenges for International Law. In: Fastenrath, U, Geiger, R, Kahn, DE, Paulus, A, von Schorlemer, S & C Vedder (eds) *From Bilateralism to Community Interest – Essays in Honour of Judge Bruno Simma.* Oxford, Oxford University Press, 1278-1297, 1285.

8   For further details *see* Rayfuse, R & SV Scott (2012) Mapping the Impact of Climate Change on International Law. In: Rayfuse, R & SV Scott (eds) *International Law in the Era of Climate Change.* Cheltenham, Edward Elgar, 3-25.

International law with multilateral agreements on the global, regional and subregional level; bilateral (and unilateral) agreements; general principles of law; customary international law; case law; and other instruments such as declarations and agendas are authoritative sources of climate law. In terms of national law, it consists of constitutional law, statutory law, common law, case law, customary law, policies, strategies and action plans and other relevant instruments. Then there is the demarcation between 'hard' and 'soft' law. While some of the sources of national and international law are obligatory, others are of a non-binding nature. Ultimately, climate law consists of the sum of legal provisions protecting the climate itself and those that protect the climate and society from the negative effects of climate change. In this light, sound lawmaking is not possible unless scientific results provide the necessary guidance.

The Intergovernmental Panel on Climate Change (IPCC) is the authoritative body to rely on when it comes to quantitative detection and attribution studies to develop impact assessments, which in turn can be used in support of adaptation planning. The IPCC provides rigorous and balanced scientific information to decision makers, and by endorsing the IPCC reports, governments acknowledge the authority of their scientific content. The work of the IPCC is meant to be policy relevant and yet policy neutral, never policy prescriptive.[9] The 2021 publication of the IPCC's Sixth Assessment Report (AR6) will most likely bring new scientific findings that provide further guidance, for instance, starting with COP26.

With the increasing possibility, through science, of predicting foreseeable events, such as extreme weather, increasing obligations rest on governments to perform duties to protect their citizens against harm. For the purpose of national legislation and regulation, it can be stated that the larger and more certain the body of evidence is that confirms, for instance, the effects of greenhouse gas (GHG) emissions, the better. In this regard, the new EU Climate Law can be viewed as a centrepiece of an effective climate protection policy. The most important projects in many nationally determined contributions (NDCs) are aimed at reducing the consumption of fossil fuels. This requires legislative efforts informed by science at the national level that guarantee internationally agreed standards for international trade and the certification of emissions.

In the international field, science informs negotiations to support ambitious interstate action; the allocation of funds to vulnerable regions, sectors and populations with the greatest risk; and a framework for compensation by those responsible to those detrimentally affected. Attribution science can be of further assistance to legislators in developing functional loss and damaged legal frameworks, the greatest obstacle to which is the complex and multicausal nature of harm, to make it possible for vulnerable countries and communities to ground entitlement for compensation. These include addressing

---

9   *See* www.ipcc.ch/organization/organization.shtml#.URelrmhpvos, last accessed 17 February 2020.

compensation for communities threatened by, for example, melting glaciers or rising sea levels caused by climate change.

Since the inception of the 2015 Paris Agreement, climate litigation has been increasingly on the rise worldwide: in the so-called South African 'Thabametsi case[10]' of *Earthlife Africa Johannesburg v. Minister of Environmental Affairs and others*,[11] the Gauteng High Court handed down a judgment regarding an environmental authorisation for a new coal-fired power station, in which it obliged the government to take account of the climate objectives of the United Nations Framework Convention on Climate Change (UNFCCC) and the Paris Agreement in their domestic decision-making processes and that national administrative regulations must be interpreted in such a way that they are consistent with international law.[12]

In *Urgenda v. Kingdom of the Netherlands*,[13] the Dutch Supreme Court relied heavily on IPCC reports to define the percentage reduction in GHG emissions that the government would need to achieve to prevent risks associated with climate change. The 2019 Urgenda judgment repeatedly makes explicit reference to the IPCC, e.g., its Fourth Assessment Report (AR4), Fifth Assessment Report (AR5) and AR5 Synthesis Report. Under the facts of the case, the court even discusses the role of the IPCC reports in obtaining insight into all aspects of climate change through scientific research. In doing so, the court acknowledges its scientific authority related to climate evidence.[14] In fact, judicial findings, as in the Urgenda or Thabametsi cases, offer enormous potential for enhancing public understanding of climate science with an educating effect.[15] Developments in statistical methods to measure and quantify the contribution of human activities to specific individual climatic events seem to make courts more susceptible to the notion of corporate responsibility for climate harm, provided that partial or contributory causation can be proved.

In the appeal of a Peruvian farmer in the case of *Lliuya v. RWE AG*[16] a German court accepted climate models as a valid source of legal evidence and ruled that the question

---

10 This was arguably the first climate litigation case on the African continent; *cf.* Conference presentation on the 'Thabametsi Case' at the International Conference on Climate Change, Responsibility and Liability, Faculty of Law, University of Graz, Austria on 8 November 2018; Ruppel, OC (forthcoming) Climate Change, Responsibility and Liability in South Africa: The Legal System, Public and Private Law Considerations. In: Hinteregger, M, Kirchengast, G, Meyer, L, Schnedl, G, Schulev-Steindl, E & K Steininger (eds) *Climate Change, Responsibility and Liability*. Baden-Baden, Nomos Law Publishers.

11 ZAGPPHC 58 (2017) 65662/16.

12 Saiger, AJ (2020) Domestic Courts and the Paris Agreement's Climate Goals: The Need for a Comparative Approach. *Transnational Environmental Law*, 9:1, 37-54, 49.

13 2015 HAZA C/09/00456689.

14 For a discussion on the role of the IPCC, see Ruppel (2013) 47-51.

15 *Cf.* Ruppel, OC, Junger, GW & KM Knutton (2020) Der Klimawandel in der Governance, Gesetzgebung und Rechtsprechung Südafrikas: Ein Überblick über die jüngsten Entwicklungen. *Zeitschrift für Umweltrecht (ZUR)* Nr. 5, 273-279.

16 OLG Hamm 5 U 15/17; LG Essen 2 O 285/15; Setzer, J & LC Vanhala (2019) Climate Change Litigation: A Review of Research on Courts and Litigants in Climate Governance. *Wiley Interdisciplinary Reviews*, 16.

whether RWE's emissions partly contributed to the harm to the plaintiff was a matter of scientific determination.[17] Climate science is critical in establishing that litigants have standing to sue (*locus standi*).[18]

In *Massachusetts v. Environmental Protection Agency*,[19] a case involving a government failure to regulate GHG emissions pursuant to an existing statutory scheme for air pollution control, the US Supreme Court ruled that the plaintiffs had standing to sue because scientific research supported the link between climate change and the coastal land, for which the state had a public trust responsibility to protect.[20] In other climate litigation cases, courts explicitly recognised that rational decisions cannot be made by administrators without access to and consideration of scientific reports addressing climate change.

4   THE NEXUS BETWEEN CLIMATE LAW AND CLIMATE SCIENCE

This brings me to the nexus of climate law and climate science as both disciplines have their own autonomy, methodology and function. Scientists argue that their opinions are objective facts and reality, while the legal process usually requires the presentation of evidence and the determination of disputes of fact and often conflicting scientific data, methodology and opinions.

Conflicting interplays have all too often been recognised between science and law as practised in the courts. On the one hand, science is criticised as setting limitations on what is provable in court and struggling with legal formalities. On the other hand, the law is accused of being overly technical in its approach and insufficiently informed by science. This may be attributable to the different standards for certainty accepted by scientists, as opposed to the legal burdens of proof applied by courts and/or the difficulty in applying scientific opinions to remedy-based legal criteria.[21] The level of certainty required by scientists is that of no less than 90%; in other words, uncertainty in results should be reduced to less than 10%. In many civil cases, a court will accept a conclusion if it has been established on the balance of probabilities or with certainty greater than 50%.[22] Thus, a regular criticism is that attribution studies are written by scientists for a scientific audience

17   Setzer & Vanhala (2019) 15.
18   Burger, M, Wentz, J, & Horton, R (2020) The Law and Science of Climate Change Attribution. *Columbia Journal of Environmental Law*, 45:1, 57-241, 67.
19   Supreme Court of the United States 2 April 2007, *Massachusetts v. EPA*, 549 US 497. Setzer & Vanhala (2019) 15; Burger et al (2020) 72.
20   Burger et al (2020) 16.
21   McEldowney, J & S McEldowney (2011) Science and Environmental Law: Collaboration across the Double Helix. *Environmental Law Review*, 13:3, 169, 173.
22   Marjanac, S & L Patton (2018) Extreme Weather Event Attribution Science and Climate Change Litigation: and Essential Step in the Causal Chain? *Journal of Energy & Natural Resources Law*, 1, 16.

that is assumed to know the terminology, concepts and confidence levels and for not being accessible to or designed for judicial use.[23]

The need arose that lawyers better understand scientific evidence. While a scientist testifying in court usually presents opinions and facts, assumptions and criteria on which they are based, it is the duty of the court to evaluate and test the accuracy thereof, as it must form its own independent judgment.[24] Analysing this dichotomy is subject to an inherent disconnect between scientists and litigation lawyers because of their different roles. Lawyers represent interests, while scientists are supposed to be neutral and impartial. Yet I argue that in order to become a joint enabler of a new climate enlightenment, scientists and lawyers must establish more formal collaborative interdisciplinary pathways to achieve and optimise impact-driven knowledge exchange. Interdisciplinary researches from both natural and social sciences beyond disciplinary boundaries must respect one another with the practical need to overcome artificial barriers while integrating a new understanding of climate sustainability.

5   Climate Justice Pathways for a New Climate Enlightenment?

At the beginning of the year 2020, approximately 7.5 billion people lived on Earth. That was around 83 million people more than one year earlier. An average of 2.6 earthlings are currently added every second if one adds the births minus the deaths. The 8-billion mark is expected to be reached in 2023.[25] These massive human populations not only contribute to the climate crisis but are, at the same time, depleting non-renewable natural resources at a very rapid rate. What does this mean on the grounds of fairness or justice, limits to the scarce resources?

In this context, climate justice pathways for a new climate enlightenment should perhaps draw on experiences from the age of enlightenment, *le siècle des lumières, das Zeitalter der Aufklärung*, in which ideas concerning God, reason, nature and humanity were synthesised into a worldview that gained wide assent and that instigated revolutionary developments.

Sapere aude, the Latin phrase meaning 'dare to know' or, more loosely, 'dare to think for yourself', became associated with the age of enlightenment, after Immanuel Kant used it in the essay 'Answering the question: What is enlightenment?' in 1784. He claimed *Sapere aude* as a leitmotif to develop theories of the application of reason in the public sphere of human affairs. Central to the enlightenment was the question of how reason can empower

---

23   Burger et al (2020) 122.

24   *PriceWaterhouseCoopers Inc and Others v. National Potato Co-operative Ltd and Another* (451/12) [2015] ZASCA 2.

25   *Cf.* www.dw.com/de/weltbevölkerung-wächst-weiter/a-51752863?maca=de-newsletter_de_themen-2076-html-newsletter, last accessed 20 May 2020.

humans to better understand the universe and improve their own living conditions. Thus, the enlightenment became critical, reforming and eventually revolutionary, evolving arbitrary, authoritarian states towards a higher form of social organisation based on natural rights and a functioning political democracy.[26]

But how is this relevant today – in the context of climate change? The answer is that human ingenuity and effort in areas such as education, innovation, technology, government, medicine and agriculture can overcome the negative influences of climate. Man is not simply subject to the necessity of nature; he/she can shape his/her own destiny as a free agent and bring about his/her destined and proper future.[27]

The name Charles-Louis de Secondat, Baron de La Brède et de Montesquieu, generally referred to as Montesquieu, combined ideals of a free society, constitutionalism and civil rights, the separation of powers and freedom of expression, the rule of law and the striving for social equality. Montesquieu was a lawyer and a scientist. He was a liberal who questioned the outdated and, at the same time, a conservative who warned of overthrowing existing laws where there was no real demand. He was both a French citizen and a citizen of the world who neither promoted nor anticipated the French Revolution.[28]

As early as 1748, in chapter 16[29] of his work *de l'esprit des lois,* Montesquieu analyses the connection between climate and law. His thesis can be summarised as follows: climate is a determinant factor of human life;[30] it has an impact on the human spirit and consequently – among other conditions – on the legal system of a society. The ideal legislator – according to Montesquieu – must anticipate the conditions of nature in order to develop society in the best possible way.

Despite well-known flaws in Montesquieu's climate theory, what does it mean for the interplay of climate law and climate science today? According to Montesquieu, legislation can either mitigate or reinforce climate-related conditions. The ideal legislator must therefore anticipate not only existing (but, where possible, also future) conditions. His attempt to scientifically justify politics and law was influenced largely by his scientific thinking. Although Montesquieu followed the tradition of liberalism in political theory, given his scientific approach to social, legal and political systems, his influence extended well beyond this tradition.[31]

---

26 *Cf.* www.britannica.com/event/Enlightenment-European-history, last accessed 20 May 2020.

27 Fleming, JR (2005) Historical Perspectives on Climate Change. Oxford, Oxford University Press, 26.

28 Lepenies, W (2017) Montesquieu: Franzose, Aufklärer, Weltbürger. Er gilt als Erfinder der Gewaltenteilung. Doch sein Werk ,Vom Geist der Gesetze' ist ein Zeugnis universaler Gelehrsamkeit; available at www.welt.de/kultur/article8549173/Franzose-Aufklaerer-Weltbuerger.html, last accessed 20 May 2020.

29 Chapter 16 *'Lois dans le rapport qu'elles ont avec la nature du climat'* = 'On the laws in their relation to the nature of the climate.'

30 Müller, R (2005) Montesquieu über Umwelt und Gesellschaft – die Klimatheorie und ihre Folgen, Sitzungsberichte der Leibniz-Sozietät, 80, 19-32.

31 *Cf.* https://plato.stanford.edu/entries/enlightenment/, last accessed 7 June 2020.

Following his approach, a new sense of climate enlightenment should place the idea of moral progress at the very top of the overall social target structures. Such moral progress should further align all human actions with universal values such as human dignity, the inherent concept of freedom, the absolute equality of all people and solidarity in terms of what we must do or what we must refrain from doing in anticipation and response to the complex and threatening climate crisis. For Montesquieu, the law relates to the necessities (*rapports nécessaires*) resulting from the nature of things (*la nature des choses*). In this light, the law should be seen analogously to the laws of nature.

While – according to Montesquieu – mankind and functioning society are dependent on various variables (*esprit general*), the climate plays a predominant role for human subsistence and survival. Men, so Montesquieu, by their care and their good laws, must make Earth a fitter home.[32] We can reshape the law in that it emerges from being reactive in nature to become proactive. This seems in line with what is stated in his encyclical letter *Laudato Si*, where Pope Francis, in 2015, emphasises the care of our common home that "human beings, endowed with intelligence, must respect the laws of nature and the delicate equilibria existing between the creatures of this world".[33]

Pope Francis goes on to say that one authoritative source of oversight and coordination is the law, which lays down rules for admissible conduct in the light of the common good. He further says that science and technology are wonderful products of God-given human creativity and that science that would offer solutions to the great issues would necessarily have to take into account the data generated by other fields of knowledge, including philosophy and social ethics.[34] Therefore, in order to pave the way for climate justice pathways, dialogue among the various sciences is likewise needed, since each can tend to become enclosed in its own language, while specialisation leads to a certain isolation and the absolutisation of its own field of knowledge.[35]

6 SCIENCE INFORMS LAW, LAW SHAPES BEHAVIOUR

Increasing climate change slows economic growth, threatens food security, exacerbates social inequalities and harbours the risk of violent conflicts and increased migration movements. We have the necessary evidence at hand, yet we remain hesitant to act. From a behavioural science perspective, the climate crisis mandates that we limit ourselves as individuals and nations for a more global common good. The constraints we are being

---

32 (XVIII.7, 289).
33 *Cf.* www.vatican.va/content/francesco/en/encyclicals/documents/papa-francesco_20150524_enciclica-lau dato-si.html, last accessed 20 May 2020.
34 Id.
35 Id.

asked to accept are experienced in the present, while the impacts of our negligence may be felt only in the future. The more distant a threat appears, the less willing we seem to take action. This should be overcome by means of a transformational shift in the way we value the capital of nature in the promotion of nature conservation and climate mitigation.

Many countries have implemented national climate policies to accomplish pledged NDCs and to contribute to the temperature objectives of the Paris Agreement on climate change. And while in 2023, the global stocktake will assess the combined effort of countries, it is already apparent that the implementation of those policies will leave a significant emission gap towards the temperature goals of well below 2 °C and 1.5 °C agreed in Paris. By 2050, the European Union, for instance, wants to be climate neutral. This is an ambitious goal that committed role models can promote. National climate protection legislation should therefore also focus more on the exemplary function of the public sector and its administration (e.g. cities and municipalities).

Moreover, many companies are prioritising action on climate change, and sustainability has become a key selling point. Yet with respect to corporate social and environmental responsibility, existing regulatory regimes are still largely inconsistent and, at worst, ineffective. Such responsibility is attached to actions before or while taking them and does not arise after the fact.[36] In order to evolve more coherent and consistent standards to regulate corporations as part of efforts to mitigate and adapt to climate change, the scope of legal obligations that states and enterprises have to defend and protect often still needs legal adjustment.

Until recently, climate law was largely the focus of diplomatic discussions, treaty negotiations and academic debates, whereas today a new corporate culture of sustainability requires new set of skills to respond to low carbon ambition. Understanding climate law must emerge as a skill set for commercial, not only environmental, attorneys, regardless of where they practise and whom they represent. So far, in legal education and training of lawyers, judges and legal practitioners, this skill set has largely fallen short, and just as much as any patent attorney needs a scientific background in addition to the legal one, the legal climate practitioner requires access to insights provided by climate science in order to be able to, inter alia, provide the best possible client advice, protect directors from unforeseen liabilities and communicate legal arguments supported by robust climate evidence.

The question arises as to how legal systems can actually contribute to framework conditions, for example, to better protect particularly vulnerable ecosystems and groups from the consequences of climate change. Legal systems are based on certainties and not

---

36 N'Djomon, A (2018) 'Le Responsabilité sociale de l'Enterprise s'inscrit dans une perspective libérale!' In: Kinhoun, E & OC Ruppel (eds) *La Question de la Responsabilité Sociale et Environnementale de L'Enterprise Perspective Africaine, Cas du Cameroun*, 39-44.

uncertainties: Written standards are to be followed, contracts must be adhered to, public documents and registers should provide legal certainty, and precise statements by the administration and the courts can be enforced.

While science can afford certain levels of uncertainty, the question is the extent to which law will be able to do so. Thus, have, for instance, the so-called 2017 Oslo Principles stated that "law is the bridge between scientific knowledge and political action". Therefore, in principle, the law must develop and adapt to new circumstances and developments. *De lege lata – de lege ferenda.* This happens, for example, through the development of new positive law and also through the adaptation or interpretation of existing legal norms through the case law of the courts. Norms, institutions or legal concepts are capable of adapting to a changing social and regulatory context. In this light, comparative climate law, legal transplants (*Rechtstransfer*) and other 'legal models or model laws' are expected to develop more rapidly where, for instance, certain 'national achievements' in climate litigation in one legal system can be 'received' in another legal system or even on supranational or international levels in a world that knows no environmental boundaries.

In order to effectively avert the climate crisis, the right degree of legal regulations and shifted incentives seems to be crucial in motivating individual and national action for more collective success. Consequently, despite the remaining scientific uncertainty, we need to stop seeing the threat posed by climate change as lying very far ahead in order to overcome a low willingness to immediately modify our behaviour in preparation for a sustainable future.[37] After all, the law depends on the statements and warnings of science. If the law reaches the limits of knowledge and thus certainty, it depends on references generated in other knowledge systems (science, economy, technology, ecology, etc.). Given the complexity and degree of uncertainty around climate change, such expert systems must serve the law to provide, where possible, reliable references. Such high levels of complexity are, of course, non-linear in nature and the types of prognosis possibilistic, probabilistic or conditional.

But although the future is open, it is not entirely arbitrary but rooted in its origins, so it is always a kind of continuation, where change is driven by megatrends. And despite remaining "climate wild cards", science must contribute to strengthening the resilience of individuals, societies and economies to systemic climate crisis phenomena. It needs to inform the law and society of what cause is expected to have which effect and which concerted effects can either be prevented or constructed and, perhaps above all, who determines what can be disregarded in the process.[38]

---

[37]   *Cf.* www.die-gdi.de/en/the-current-column/article/parallels-between-the-corona-pandemic-and-climate-change-1/, last accessed 7 June 2020.

[38]   Renn, O (2019) Gefühlte Wahrheiten: Orientierung in Zeiten postfaktischer Verunsicherung, 2 Ausgabe, Verlag Barbara Budrich, 26.

Crossing the divide between law and science raises the inevitable question of whether the legal profession is skilled enough to address the scientific needs of the legal system. After all, science and law have always coexisted, and it is science that can enlighten the legal profession in revealing the truth to the courts in complex matters and by means of scientific advancement impacting the administration of justice.

In the process, the independence of scientists from governmental influence and political agendas must be preserved so as to avoid creating the perception that they are working towards preconceived political goals or agendas.[39] Science indicates a rapid need to address the climate crisis. Science has answers to the issues before us. We must let science inform the discourse, which in turn inspires laws, policies and procedures that can deal with the climate crisis and enlighten a system that ensures that we 'leave no one behind'. Solutions to the current COVID-19 crisis need to be aligned with those of the climate crisis for a global transformation towards more sustainability, resilience, equity, justice and peace.[40] While the consequences of climate change have the potential to fuel conflicts, peace is acutely endangered, having a negative impact on social justice and equality. Thus, the nexus between climate change and human security is gaining more and more importance. Damaged ecosystems and biodiversity loss threaten food security, with the poorest and most vulnerable suffering the most. Therefore, we need to increase our resilience. On the one hand, climate change has a threat potential comparable to a world war. On the other hand, this threat does not divide the world but should unite all people, states, corporations, etc., regardless of origin, location or jurisdiction.

As such, Montesquieu's considerations of natural law and its inherent coexistence with the environment must be seen as a binding constraint for all forms of human activity and should therefore be so managed as to reflect its biophysical, ethical and economic value. And, ultimately, in the achievement of natural justice the law has a prominent role to play in order to prevent the world from overshoot.

7   OUTLOOK[41]

[...] *und um meine besondere Ehrerbietung zu erweisen, erlaube ich mir an dieser Stelle ein paar abschließende Worte in deutscher Sprache: In Zeiten der Klimakrise steht das Recht*

---

39   McEldowney & McEldowney (2011) 194.

40   *See* Jayaram, D (2020) Climate Diplomacy Can Help Tackle the COVID-19 Crisis. *Climate Diplomacy Magazine*, at https://climate-diplomacy.org/magazine/cooperation/climate-diplomacy-can-help-tackle-covid-19-crisis, last accessed 25 January 2021.

41   Translations from German: [...] and to pay my special respect, I will take the liberty at this point of saying a few concluding words in German: [...]: In times of climate crisis, the law is increasingly caught up in the tension between risk, complexity and uncertainty. If climate change continues to intensify in the coming decades, the danger of abrupt, irreversible climate changes with very high risk (tipping points) will increase. I have

im zunehmenden Spannungsgefüge von Risiko, Komplexität und Ungewissheit. Verstärkt sich der Klimawandel in den kommenden Jahrzehnten weiter, steigt die Gefahr von abrupten, unumkehrbaren Klimaänderungen mit sehr hohem Risiko (Kipppunkte).

Ich habe versucht auf die Frage einzugehen, wie das Recht künftig angepasst, mit Hilfe der Wissenschaft, bessere Rahmenbedingungen schaffen kann, um zum Beispiel besonders verwundbare Ökosysteme und Gruppen vor den Folgen des Klimawandels besser schützen zu können. In vielen Ländern der Erde ist das Klimaschutzrecht auf dem Vormarsch und führt zwangsläufig bereits zu mehr Rechtssicherheit bei zunehmender klimabedingter Unsicherheit.[42] Es gibt bereits viele positive und proaktive Maßnahmen, die die Anpassung und Minderung des Klimawandels regulatorisch behandeln.[43] Wichtig erscheint dabei jedoch keinesfalls die Unsicherheitsdynamik aus dem Auge zu verlieren. In der Klimakrise ist das Recht von den Stellungnahmen und Warnungen der Wissenschaft abhängig, insbesondere dort, wo die Wissenschaft vor einer Risikosituation warnt. Wenn das Recht an die Grenzen

---

tried to address the question of how the law can be adapted in the future, with the help of science, to create better framework conditions, for example, to better protect particularly vulnerable ecosystems and groups from the consequences of climate change. In many countries around the world, climate change law is on the rise, inevitably already leading to more legal certainty in the face of increasing climate-related uncertainty. There are already many positive and proactive measures that address climate change adaptation and mitigation in regulatory terms. However, it seems important not to lose sight of the uncertainty dynamics. In the climate crisis, the law is dependent on the opinions and warnings of science, especially where science warns of risk situations. When the law reaches the limits of knowledge, it has to resort to other reference systems. Scientific expert systems can provide the law with references that it does not possess itself. The scientific recommendations for action of the Intergovernmental Panel on Climate Change have condensed in a worrying way in recent years.

Therefore, it is now more important than ever to prioritise climate protection in terms of security policy, to implement it under international law, to make it justiciable worldwide and to endow it with greater constitutional quality at the national level. In short, 'a policy of small steps at a time when there is no time left will in any case not be sufficient to meet the challenges of the Anthropocene in time'. Against this background, a policy of large steps can open up transformation perspectives (such as the European Green Deal), which in the future will combine both economic and ecological aspects of natural capital profitably as a valuable commodity, which needs a price tag while actually being priceless. With the founding of ClimLaw, the Graz Research Center for Climate Law, a platform has been created where law and climate protection can meet, inform and discuss discursively, transnationally and transdisciplinary in the future. I congratulate Austria, Styria, Graz and the venerable university there with its law faculty on this seminal decision, and I congratulate my esteemed colleague, Professor Dr. Schulev-Steindl – dear Eva – as well as our colleagues at ClimLaw on this outstanding academic opportunity to examine the law in the context of climate change and to further develop it in the service of humanity.

42   *Cf.* Ruppel, OC (2014) Climate Change Law and Policy in the African Union and Selected African Countries. In: Spier, J & U Magnus (eds) *Climate Change Remedies: Injunctive Relief and Criminal Law Responses.* The Hague, Eleven International Publishing, 191-220; Ruppel, OC (2015) Climate Change, Law and Development in Africa: A Reflection on Selected Aspects, Relations and Responses. In: König, D, Koch, H-J, Sanden, J & R Verheyen (eds) *Legal Regimes for Environmental Protection, Governance for Climate Change and Ocean Resources.* Leiden, Brill | Nijhoff, 89-125.

43   Rumble, O (2019) Climate Change Legislative Development on the African Continent. In: Kameri-Mbote, P, Paterson, A, Ruppel, OC, Orubebe, BB & ED Kam Yogo (eds) *Law | Environment | Africa.* Recht und Verfassung in Afrika, Bd. 38. Baden-Baden, Nomos Law Publishers, 33-60, 43.

des Wissens stößt, muss es auf andere Referenzsysteme zurückgreifen. Expertensysteme können dem Recht Referenzen zur Verfügung zu stellen, die es selbst nicht besitzt. Die wissenschaftlichen Handlungsempfehlungen des Weltklimarats haben sich in den vergangenen Jahren auf besorgniserregende Art und Weise verdichtet.

Daher gilt es heute mehr denn je, den Klimaschutz sicherheitspolitisch zu priorisieren, völkerrechtlich umzusetzen, weltweit justiziabel zu machen und auf nationaler Ebene mit größerer Verfassungsqualität auszustatten. Kurzum, ,eine Politik der kleinen Schritte in einer Zeit, in der keine Zeit mehr verbleibt, wird jedenfalls nicht ausreichen, um den Herausforderungen im Anthropozän rechtzeitig zu begegnen'.[44] Vor diesem Hintergrund kann eine Politik der großen Schritte Transformationsperspektiven (wie z.B. der europäische Green Deal) eröffnen, welche künftig zugleich ökomische und ökologische Aspekte natürlichen Kapitals gewinnbringend als wertvolles Gut kombinieren, was zwar ein Preisschild braucht, eigentlich aber unbezahlbar ist.

Durch die Gründung von ClimLaw, dem Graz Research Center for Climate Law, wurde eine Plattform geschaffen, wo sich Recht und Klimaschutz künftig diskursiv, grenzüberschreitend und transdisziplinär begegnen, informieren und auseinandersetzen können. Ich beglückwünsche Österreich, die Steiermark, Graz und die dortige altehrwürdige Universität mit seiner Rechtsfakultät zu dieser zukunftsträchtigen Entscheidung und gratuliere meiner verehrten Kollegin, Professor Dr. Schulev-Steindl – liebe Eva – sowie unseren Kolleginnen und Kollegen bei ClimLaw zu dieser herausragenden akademischen Möglichkeit, das Recht im Zeichen des Klimawandels zu untersuchen und im Dienste der Menschheit fortzuentwickeln.

BIBLIOGRAPHY

Bristow, Enlightenment, https://plato.stanford.edu/entries/enlightenment/ (29 August 2017).

Burger/Wentz/Horton, The Law and Science of Climate Change Attribution. Columbia Journal of Environmental Law 2020, 57.

Deutsche Welle, Weltbevölkerung wächst weiter, www.dw.com/de/weltbev%C3%B6lkerung-w%C3%A4chst-weiter/a-51752863?maca=de-newsletter_de_themen-2076-html-newsletter (20 December 2019).

---

44   Ruppel, OC & A Wulff (2016) Klimawandel und Energiesicherheit im Anthropozän: Afrika im Lichte des Pariser Klimaschutzabkommens. *Auslandsinformationen: Klima. Energie. Sicherheit.* 2/2016. Berlin, Konrad-Adenauer-Stiftung, 48-63, 61.

Duignan, Enlightenment, www.britannica.com/event/Enlightenment-European-history (15 March 2021).

Fleming, Historical Perspectives on Climate Change (2005).

Fuhrmann/Kuhn, Behavioural Changes in Times of Crisis: Parallels between the Corona Pandemic and Climate Change, www.die-gdi.de/uploads/media/German_Development_Institute_Fuhrmann_Kuhn_01.04.2020.pdf (1 April 2020).

IPCC, About the IPCC, www.ipcc.ch/organization/organization.shtml#.URelrmhpvos (17 February 2021).

Jayaram, Climate Diplomacy Can Help Tackle the COVID-19 Crisis, https://climate-diplomacy.org/magazine/cooperation/climate-diplomacy-can-help-tackle-covid-19-crisis (4 May 2020).

Lepenies, Montesquieu: Franzose, Aufklärer, Weltbürger, www.welt.de/kultur/article8549173/Franzose-Aufklaerer-Weltbuerger.html (20 July 2020).

Marjanac/Patton, Extreme Weather Event Attribution Science and Climate Change Litigation: An Essential Step in the Causal Chain? Journal of Energy & Natural Resources Law 2018, 265.

McEldowney/McEldowney, Science and Environmental Law: Collaboration across the Double Helix, Environmental Law Review 2011, 169.

Müller, Montesquieu über Umwelt und Gesellschaft – die Klimatheorie und ihre Folgen, Sitzungsberichte der Leibniz-Sozietät 80, 2005, 19.

N'Djomon, Le Responsabilité sociale de l'Enterprise s'inscrit dans une perspective libérale! in *Kinhoun/Ruppel* (eds), La Question de la Responsabilité Sociale et Environnementale de L'Enterprise Perspective Africaine, Cas du Cameroun (2018).

Perthes, The Corona Crisis and International Relations: Open Questions, Tentative Assumptions, www.swp-berlin.org/en/publication/the-corona-crisis-and-international-relations-open-questions-tentative-assumptions/ (31 March 2020).

Rayfuse/Scott, Mapping the Impact of Climate Change on International Law, in *Rayfuse/Scott* (eds) International Law in the Era of Climate Change (2012).

Renn, Gefühlte Wahrheiten: Orientierung in Zeiten postfaktischer Verunsicherung² (2019).

Rumble, Climate Change Legislative Development on the African Continent, in *Kameri-Mbote/Paterson/Ruppel/Orubebe/Kam Yogo* (eds), Law | Environment | Africa. Recht und Verfassung in Afrika (2019).

Ruppel, Climate Change, Law and Development in Africa: A Reflection on Selected Aspects, Relations and Responses, in *König/Koch/Sanden/Verheyen* (eds), Legal Regimes for Environmental Protection, Governance for Climate Change and Ocean Resources (2015).

Ruppel, Climate Change Law and Policy in the African Union and Selected African Countries, in *Spier/Magnus* (eds), Climate Change Remedies: Injunctive Relief and Criminal Law Responses (2014).

Ruppel, Climate Change, Responsibility and Liability in South Africa: The Legal System, Public and Private Law Considerations, in *Hinteregger/Kirchengast/Meyer et al* (eds), Climate Change, Responsibility and Liability (forthcoming).

Ruppel, Intersections of Law and Cooperative Global Climate Governance – Challenges in the Anthropocene, in *Ruppel/Roschmann/Ruppel-Schlichting* (eds), Climate Change: International Law and Global Governance Volume I: Legal Responses and Global Responsibility (2013).

Ruppel, Wasser und Land – Brennpunkte innerhalb der Entwicklungsgemeinschaft des südlichen Afrikas (SADC), in *Reder/Pfeifer* (eds), Kampf um Ressourcen. Weltordnung zwischen Konkurrenz und Kooperation – Globale Solidarität, Schritte zu einer neuen Weltkultur (2012).

Ruppel/Junger/Knutton, Der Klimawandel in der Governance, Gesetzgebung und Rechtsprechung Südafrikas: Ein Überblick über die jüngsten Entwicklungen, Zeitschrift für Umweltrecht 2020, 273.

Ruppel/Wulff, Klimawandel und Energiesicherheit im Anthropozän: Afrika im Lichte des Pariser Klimaschutzabkommens. Auslandsinformationen: Klima. Energie. Sicherheit. (2016).

Saiger, Domestic Courts and the Paris Agreement's Climate Goals: The Need for a Comparative Approach, Transnational Environmental Law 2020, 37.

Schrijver, The Impact of Climate Change: Challenges for International Law, in *Fastenrath/Geiger/Kahn et al* (eds), From Bilateralism to Community Interest – Essays in Honour of Judge Bruno Simma (2011).

Setzer/Vanhala, Climate Change Litigation: A Review of Research on Courts and Litigants in Climate Governance, Wiley Interdisciplinary Reviews 2019/10.

Tomuschat, Risk and Security in International Law, in *Hestermeyer/König/Matz-Lück et al* (eds), Coexistence, Cooperation and Solidarity: Liber Amicorum Rüdiger Wolfrum (2012).

Vatican, Encyclical Letter Laudato Si' of Holy Father Francis on Care for our Common Home, www.vatican.va/content/francesco/en/encyclicals/documents/papa-francesco_20150524_enciclica-laudato-si.html (last accessed 20 May 2020).

Cases

Germany

Landgericht Essen 15 December 2016, *Lliuya v. RWE AG*, 2 O 285/15.

Oberlandesgericht Hamm 30 November 2017, *Lliuya v. RWE AG*, 5 U 15/17.

The Netherlands

District Court of the Hague 24 June 2015, *Urgenda Foundation v. The State of the Netherlands*, HAZA C/09/00456689.

South Africa

Supreme Court of Appeal of South Africa 4 March 2015, *Price Waterhouse Coopers Inc and Others v. National Potato Co-Operative Limited*, 451/12 [2015] ZASCA 2.

High Court of South Africa 8 March 2017, *Earthlife Africa Johannesburg v. Minister of Environmental Affairs and Others*, ZAGPPHC 58 (2017) 65662/16.

United States

Supreme Court of the United States 2 April 2007, *Massachusetts v. EPA*, 549 US 497.

Against the Taming of the Spinners – On the National Goal of Climate Protection [*]

Lecture at the Opening Symposium 'Clim Law Graz – Research Center for Climate Law'

Ferdinand Kerschner

Thank you very, very much for the really honourable invitation to speak. Let me begin with a saying by the French philosopher Edgar Morin: "If you constantly sacrifice the essential to the urgent, you forget the urgency of the essential." This is a very clear picture of the climate crisis. With the foundation of the Climate Law Center, the Karl-Franzens-University Graz, where I was also briefly a visiting professor a long time ago, has dedicated itself to the urgency of the essential. The University of Graz and the head of the Center, Prof. Dr. Eva Schulev-Steindl, and her team are to be congratulated most warmly on the foundation of the Center. Good luck on the way to a sustainable climate protection law!

The corona crisis, which is still ongoing, is also essential and urgent, but the climate crisis is even more essential and has long been urgent for humanity. The climate crisis is the greatest challenge of our century.[1] Why is this so? Above all, my, that is the older, generation has destroyed more of the environment and climate than all other generations before it together. Of course, the large-scale destruction of the environment and dramatically rapid climate change are offset by many positive achievements. The former, i.e. the ever-increasing climate change, is not seen by many as such, but more and more people, especially climate scientists, who are, unfortunately, often and predominantly dismissed as crackpots by politics, business and industry, see it as the greatest challenge of our century.[2] Ninety-nine percent of climate scientists assume that climate change is anthropogenic. The designation of scientists as crackpots or the dismissal of them as crackpots also justifies the title of my lecture. We were and are enormously arrogant towards the developing and emerging countries, but also, and all the more so, towards all future generations together. Let me start with a frequent objection to climate protection:

---

[*]   Compare the title already by *Kerschner/Schulev-Steindl*, Editorial, RdU 2019/1,1.

[1]   *See also Kerschner*, Nach der Corona-Krise mitten in der Klimakrise, Unterschiede und gemeinsame Chancen und Gefahren, RdU 2020/49, 93 ff.

[2]   Compare *Bergthaler/Kerschner/Schulev-Steindl*, Was Österreich braucht, ist Klimaschutz! Editorial, RdU 2018/1, 1.

the EU, as a whole, accounts for only 10% of CO_2 emissions. However, this is 10% of total CO_2 emissions, and it is overlooked that the EU, and the industrialised countries, in general, have a significant role model effect vis-à-vis the developing and emerging countries. *If we do not change our behaviour, we cannot demand the same behaviour from the developing and emerging countries.*

In the corona crisis, science and politics made the right decision, namely science-oriented and science-based, based on facts and data. This is now the opportunity for politicians to act immediately on the basis of knowledge in the climate crisis and to set the right course in the climate crisis. Instead of the decision makers in Austria and the EU setting an example in the climate crisis, as previously demanded, following the polluter-pays principle, I believe that despite all the assertions to the contrary and despite some laudable exceptions and positive approaches, the idea of growth is already quite present again. One need only look at the advertisements in the media; the idea of growth is once again pressing and a priority for many. **The danger of the frenzy of exclusively calculating thinking** (*Martin Heidegger*) **is threatening.** This must not happen again. So the crackpots must be heard here too, and lawyers must and should be crackpots too. They should also hear all other science madmen. The market economy in which we live is, moreover, highly flexible, but the right legal framework is still lacking at the moment, and it still needs to be shaped and implemented.

But for this, we do not have to abolish the market economy, capitalism, as some people are certainly demanding. *We must reverse the polarity of the market economy.* To do this, we need realistic and pragmatic legal bulwarks, such as the climate law center in Graz, which will provide the government with a basis and decisive help in the climate emergency declared by parliament. *My thesis is that climate protection in Austria, but probably also in most other EU Member States, has not yet or not sufficiently arrived in law or the legal system.* At the same time, we in Austria would actually have a very good starting position, which, as will be shown, is not shared by the courts.

What is this about? We have a *national goal of environmental protection,*[3] and it is undisputed and undeniable that *climate protection is part of environmental protection* and part of sustainability and health protection. Climate change affects almost all environmental media. We are, therefore, actually in a better starting position than in Germany, where there is not yet a national goal of sustainable development. For Germany, such a national goal is urgently demanded[4] by the former president of the German Federal Constitutional Court, *Hans-Jürgen Papier,* in his book *Die Warnung (The Warning).* We would therefore not really need an actual national goal of climate protection, although this would, of course, do no harm. What would still help, however, would be a basic right to climate protection,

---

3   *See Kerschner* (Ed.), Staatsziel Umweltschutz (1996).
4   *The warning – How the rule of law is being undermined* (2019)[3] 235 ff.

because this would be linked to a subjective right of the individual. So we have a national climate protection target, but many people say *yes* to it, not only *yes*, but *yes, but* [...]! There are also many reasons among lawyers and judges why climate change is denied. I would now like to go into this in more detail.

Many people still deny the climate crisis and its significance. There are many mechanisms of repression; I would just like to point out a few of the most important ones. Many people deny the climate crisis, as such, at least as one that was decisively caused by humans, and this despite the fact that *ninety-nine percent* of climate scientists (!) affirm and prove the anthropogenic influence. Especially in the time of the corona crisis, we have noticed how quickly CO_2 emissions are being reduced. Although many look on, they are of the opinion that there are more important things to do and that climate protection is very abstract at all, rather than prescribing concrete courses of action. This is something we have to fight against decisively. Climate protection must be supported by everyone and must cover all human behaviour. This is also legally suggested by Article 191 TFEU. It is about the *polluter-pays principle*,[5] and it is precisely our older generation that is the main cause of the climate crisis.

What also still prevails in many cases is that we do not want to change. We know about climate change and that our children and grandchildren will flee from storms and droughts, but we are far too busy. Hopefully, the corona crisis has given us more food for thought in this respect too.

There is one last reason for denial or repression mentioned here: *especially our generation has produced many technical and other positive achievements and has achieved a lot. Therefore, it is psychologically explainable that we do not want to recognise that we have massively destroyed our environment, and the climate has been considerably disadvantaged.* Global warming can no longer be denied. This also explains why more and more colleagues of my generation see Greta Thunberg as an enemy. It is so difficult to see that the achievements have also caused great, indeed the greatest, sacrifices in terms of the environment and climate.

I now come a little closer legally to the Austrian Federal Constitutional Law Sustainability and comprehensive environmental protection. Who of us really knows what this Federal Constitutional Law really says? I would like to quote exactly § 1 of the Federal Constitutional Law:

> The Republic of Austria (federal government, provinces and municipalities) is committed to the principle of sustainability in the use of natural resources in order to ensure the best possible quality of life for future generations.

---

5   *See Wagner* in *Wagner* (Ed.), Umwelt- und Anlagenrecht, Band I: Interdisziplinäre Grundlagen und Anlagenrecht[2] (2021) 95 f; *Stangl* in *Wagner* (Ed.), Umwelt- und Anlagenrecht 194 ff.

We have already heard that sustainability also means climate protection. Climate worth living in is a natural resource. Even clearer is § 3:

(1) The Republic of Austria (federal government, provinces and municipalities) is committed to comprehensive environmental protection.

(2) Comprehensive environmental protection is the protection of the natural environment as the basis of human life against harmful effects. Comprehensive environmental protection consists, in particular, of measures to keep the air, water and soil clean and to avoid disturbances caused by noise.

Comprehensive environmental protection also includes climate protection.[6] Climate protection damage is also included in § 3 (2), and it does not include an exhaustive list of measures, but it might be useful to expressly include climate protection here. Given this starting point, we could actually be very satisfied if this were to be real legal implementation. We will see that, unfortunately, these consequences have not yet been implemented by the Constitutional Court (VfGH).

What are these *normative consequences*? I have once[7] tried to analyse the decisive normative consequences in more detail: the most important aspect of the state's goal of environmental protection (including climate protection) is that it is a *mandate for action for all state organs*, i.e. not only for the administration but also for legislation and for the courts, including the Constitutional Court! Let us record that here. If you take the trouble to examine the judicates of all the supreme courts to see how far climate protection is present there, you will find that the Supreme Court in Civil and Criminal Matters (OGH) has no entry on climate protection at all, more then the Administrative Court and in some cases the Constitutional Court as well.

The next normative effect, which would be very important: *In the case of blatant violation of laws against this state objective, these laws would have to be unconstitutional.* Furthermore, the state goal of environmental protection would always have to be weighed against other fundamental rights. What I consider to be decisive in practice, but unfortunately has not been seen as such so far, *the state goal of climate protection must be taken into account in the interpretation, even in the case of dubious interpretation, in accordance with the constitution.* In environmental protection, one could, transferred from criminal law, speak of *in dubio pro natura* and in climate protection of *in dubio pro clima*.

The last important normative consequence would be that climate protection is *also* seen *as public interest in the* interpretation of laws. After all, in laws, it is often seen – and

---

6   See *Kerschner*, VfGH 3. Piste und juristische Methode: Verfassungskonforme Auslegung verfassungswidrig? RdU 2017/129, 190.
7   See *Kerschner* in *Kerschner (Ed)*, Staatsziel Umweltschutz (1996) 1 ff.

we will see this right away with the Aviation Act – that climate protection is not yet explicitly mentioned.

The *normative effects of the government's climate protection goal* have been demonstrated, and the planned third runway at Vienna's Schwechat Airport in 2017 has, so to speak, taken an oath. The Federal Administrative Court[8] rejected the construction of the third runway based on a weighing of interests. The court based its decision primarily on the national goal of climate, environmental and soil protection. This concerns a passage in § 71 of the Austrian Aviation Act, which states that *"the permit shall only be granted if there are no other public interests that stand in the way"*. The main question was whether climate protection interests are also such other public interests. The Federal Administrative Court has affirmed this.

The Austrian Constitutional Court[9] denied this within a very short time – only half a year later – on the grounds that this 128-page decision was *arbitrary (!)* with the argument that climate protection was not explicitly mentioned as public interest in the Aviation Act. In my opinion, *this decision* of the Constitutional Court was and is clearly *politically oriented*. The political pressure to build this third runway was simply too great. Not a single methodological argumentation spoke in favour of this result, and the accusation of arbitrariness by the Constitutional Court was almost arbitrary for me.[10]

The Federal Administrative Court (BVwG 23 March 2018, W 109 2000 179-1) was then bound by the decision of the Constitutional Court and had to authorise the third runway, albeit under many conditions.

The Administrative Court (VwGH 6 March 2019, Ro 2018/03/0031) was also forced to comment on this again, focusing on the environmental impact assessment procedure, which was also necessary here, and – very pleasingly – at least in principle affirmed that climate protection must also be taken into account in environmental impact assessment procedures, namely not only the *microclimate but also the macroclimate (!)*. It has made a restriction, especially for flight operations, because in the opinion of the Administrative Court, the emission certificate system is exclusive, and therefore climate protection is not to be taken into account beyond that. **But this argument of exclusivity is also nowhere in the law.**[11] The fatal consequence of the Constitutional Court's ruling is, however, that this Federal Constitutional Law on Climate Protection has become an alibi norm, because according to it, climate protection is relevant only if the legislature refers back to it. Thus,

---

8   BVwG 2 February 2017, W 109 2000 179-1.
9   VfGH 29 June 2017, E 875/2017.
10 *Kerschner*, VfGH 3. Piste und juristische Methode: Verfassungskonforme Auslegung verfassungswidrig? RdU 2017/129, 190ff; *Kerschner*, Klimaschutz aus umweltrechtlicher, insbesondere auch aus völkerrechts-konformer Sicht, RdU 2019/35, 49ff.
11 For more details *see* Kirchengast/Madner/Schulev-Steindl/Steininger/Hofer/Hollaus, RdU 2020, 76 ff.

according to this situation, the legislature decides whether the constitutional state goal of climate protection is valid or not. That is incomprehensible!

It is to be hoped that the Constitutional Court will abandon this view, but it will not be easy to resolve or get out of the dilemma. There are also new appointments to the Constitutional Court, and it is to be hoped that this will also lead to a different, more lawful view of the Constitutional Court.

We come back to the *connection with the current corona crisis*, which has resulted in a very poor economic and budgetary situation. My fear is – and I really do see dark clouds gathering here – that the previous government's idea of a renaissance of the idea of a *new state goal* will arise. This plan was about a *national goal of international competitiveness*. In my view, at the time, it was almost a declaration of war on climate and environmental protection. What was it about?

A 'Federal Constitutional Law on State Goals' was planned, i.e. no longer just comprehensive environmental protection and sustainability. A new § 3a was to be introduced, and it said: *"The Republic of Austria is committed to a competitive business location as a prerequisite for growth and employment."* This discussion about such a state target can, as I said, now come up again, even boil up. There were also explanatory comments on this proposal at the time, and it was even said that the state has a *duty to guarantee the ability to work and run a business (!)*. I do not know whether people were aware of what such a guarantee obligation means, namely that the state should really be obliged to achieve sufficient earning capacity and business capability. Such goals are enormously difficult to achieve, and if the state does not achieve these goals, official liability may well be the consequence. At the time, I, along with others, massively opposed such a state target and thought that the ecological lamb Hainburg should be sacrificed and slaughtered on the altar of the third runway so that industry and the economy would once again have completely free rein. The aim of this new state goal was clearly to prevent a decision such as that of the Federal Administrative Court on the third runway. The argument of the proponents of such a state goal was that a weighing of interests must always be carried out anyway, and such a weighing of interests is also provided for in the TFEU. In my opinion, this should be viewed quite critically and naturally also applies to the renaissance of this idea.

Why? *We have the basic rights of property and freedom of employment as the foundation of a free-market economy anyway*, and so far, this basic right has been limited by the state's goals of environmental protection, climate protection and sustainability, at least if these state goals are interpreted correctly. I believe that the planned new state objective is intended quite deliberately to break down the restrictions on these two fundamental rights of property and freedom of employment, to *paralyse* them, as it were. We could perhaps express this here metaphorically in a formula: if the national objective of protecting the climate and the environment is rated 1 and the new planned national objective is also rated 1, then all we need to do is subtract: 1-1=0! And then the paralysed state goals no longer have the effect that the basic rights to property and freedom of employment are in this respect unlimited, i.e. no longer have any limitation as they do now. At that time, I have also explained again and again and have also now connected with an *appeal to the youth: do not put up with this; it is about your future!*

The demonstrations of the *Fridays for Future* movement are, I believe, on the right track anyway. In my opinion, one must, of course, always fight against such tendencies *by democratic means* in a democratic constitutional state.

I will now come to a conclusion, namely the future scope of the Climate Law Center. It is about the meaningful *transformation of the current climate protection law.*[12] I would like to point out that, of course, regulatory law is necessary, but I believe that *market-based instruments of climate protection will also be very useful and necessary.* The idea behind them is that *in a market economy, market-based instruments are most effective, and there is a simple principle at stake here: the burden on the climate must bring material disadvantages and must be expensive. Climate-friendly behaviour must bring material advantages, profits.* In my view, there is no need for anything more than this principle, and I have already mentioned that the economy is flexible enough to implement it. Admittedly, some businesses and some industries will go under, but new, completely different ones will emerge. I would like to give just one example of the *charging of climate costs,* which is of great concern to us Austrians, namely the regulation of *motorised private transport.* As our earlier studies have already shown, it is necessary here – but has not yet been successful because transport is Austria's most sacred cow – *to charge costs to motorised private transport depending on the number of kilometres and emissions.* Those who drive more and produce more emissions must also pay more. The issue at stake is, therefore, tolls on motorised private transport.

An objection that was raised immediately was that it would make transport more expensive, making products more expensive, and that this would be at the expense of consumers. I am firmly convinced that this is precisely the aim, namely that regional organic products will become cheaper and will therefore be more likely to be bought than products from faraway countries. I would, of course, mention the CO_2 tax, which I regard as the most important instrument for charging costs, but this is a separate chapter that must be linked to an eco-bonus. I do not want to go into that in more detail here.

Lastly, the view: Let me quote Pope Francis from the *encyclical Laudato si*: "The alliance of economy and technology ultimately clings to everything that is not its immediate interest." It is now up to science to change the immediate interests of business and technology accordingly. Business and technology are flexible enough. Ultimately, what is

---

12   *See Bergthaler/Kerschner/Schulev-Steindl*, Editorial: Ein Winter- (aber auch Sommer-) Märchen oder auch mehr? RdU 2020/1, 1.

at stake is an eco-social market economy and environmentally and climate-friendly technologies. One last sentence to conclude: climate protection also, and especially, needs a strong legal voice. The Climate Law Center in Graz will be such a strong voice; I am sure of it, and I wish it every success.

BIBLIOGRAPHY AND SELECTED LITERATURE RELATED TO CLIMATE-PROTECTION LAW

Bergthaler/Kerschner/Schulev-Steindl, Was Österreich braucht, ist Klimaschutz! Editorial, RdU 2018/1, 1.

Bergthaler/Kerschner/Schulev-Steindl, Editorial: Ein Winter- (aber auch Sommer-) Märchen oder auch mehr? RdU 2020/1, 1.

Damohorsky/Proelss/Stejskal (eds), Adaption to climate changes from the perspective of law (2019).

Ennöckl, Wie kann das Recht das Klima schützen? ÖJZ 2020, 41.

Fitz/Ennöckl, Klimaschutzrecht, in *Ennöckl/Raschauer/Wessely* (eds), Handbuch Umweltrecht[3] (2019) 757.

Frenz, Grundzüge des Klimaschutzrechts (2020).

Kerschner, Klimaschutz aus umweltrechtlicher, insbesondere auch aus völkerrechtskonformer Sicht, RdU 2019/35, 49.

Kerschner, Nach der Corona-Krise mitten in der Klimakrise, Unterschiede und gemeinsame Chancen und Gefahren, RdU 2020/49, 93.

Kerschner (ed), Staatsziel Umweltschutz (1996).

Kerschner, VfGH 3. Piste und juristische Methode: Verfassungskonforme Auslegung verfassungswidrig? RdU 2017/129, 190.

Kerschner/Schulev-Steindl, Editorial, RdU 2019/1, 1.

Kirchengast/Schulev-Steindl/Schnedl (eds), Klimaschutzrecht zwischen Wunsch und Wirklichkeit (2018).

Schulev-Steindl, Klimaklagen: Ein Trend erreicht Österreich, ecolex 2021/7, 17.

Wagner (ed), Umwelt- und Anlagenrecht, Band I: Interdisziplinäre Grundlagen[2] (2021).

CASES

BVwG 2 February 2017, W 109 2000 179-1.8/1, 1.

VfGH 29 June 2017, E 875/2017.

It Is Not the Winning But the Taking Part That Counts

The Symbolic and Indirect Effects of Strategic Climate Litigation

Carlotta Garofalo

Climate lawsuits have become a global phenomenon, cutting across the five continents.[1] Lately, the humanization of climate litigation, that is, the trend of filing cases on behalf of vulnerable groups who are already affected by climate change and who seek greater protection, has increasingly drawn media attention.[2] However, the enthusiastic storytelling on high-profile climate lawsuits often overlooks a disappointing fact, namely, that they are hardly won.

On the bright side, victory in court is not all that matters in a climate lawsuit. While influencing the behavior of key actors, such as states and high-emitting companies is the ultimate purpose of strategic climate litigation, individual climate cases can address a variety of intermediate but significant steps in the overall process. In particular, strategic climate lawsuits might contribute by broadening the citizens' right to access to justice, giving credibility to scientific facts, drawing attention to human and social problems, starting a debate on a legal issue, and boosting international negotiations.[3] In other words, the idea of filing a climate lawsuit in a legally uncertain or even hostile environment still makes sense if one thinks of its broader strategic aims.

Just as with other political and legal battles for advancing human rights protection, the success of strategic climate litigation in creating social and political change will depend on time and existing social pressures.[4] From this perspective, the unsuccessful outcome

---

1   *UN Environment/Columbia University, Sabin Center for Climate Change Law*, The Status of Climate Change Litigation: A Global Review (2017); *Setzer/Byrnes*, Global Trends in Climate Litigation: A 2020 Snapshot, Policy Report (2020).

2   *Peel/Osofsky*, A Rights Turn in Climate Change Litigation? Transnational Environmental Law 2018, 37.

3   *Batros/Khan*, Thinking Strategically about Climate Litigation, www.openglobalrights.org/thinking-strategically-about-climate-litigation/ (28 June 2020); *Vanhala*, Legal Opportunity Structure and the Paradox of Legal Mobilization by the Environmental Movement in the UK, Law & Society Review 2012/46, 523; *Wonneberger/Vliegenthart*, Agenda-Setting Effects of Climate Change Litigation: Interrelations Across Issue Levels, Media, and Politics in the Case of Urgenda Against the Dutch Government, Environmental Communication 2012, 1; *Wewerinke-Singh/Salili*, Between Negotiations and Litigation: Vanuatu's Perspective on Loss and Damage from Climate Change, Climate Policy 2020, 681.

4   *Duffy*, Strategic Human Rights Litigation: Understanding and Maximising Impact (2018) 40 ff. The author mentions many examples in which specific political circumstances inhibited the immediate impact of

of many cases occasions no surprise when considering that climate litigation, especially in the form of a global mobilization of rights, is quite a new trend. The idea of suing governments and companies for their responsibilities concerning climate change, while already common in the USA and Australia at the beginning of the 2000s, took roughly ten more years to spread to the other continents.

Moreover, despite having now become a trend, the legal grounds of climate lawsuits are far from being settled. This is because climate change, owing to its temporal and spatial complexities, clashes with legal institutions, which were built on the assumption of a relatively stable human environment. According to Elizabeth Fisher,[5] two prominent reasons why climate change is *legally disruptive* are the dispersion of its causes and consequences and its potential to create social conflict. However, the same disruptive aspects that make climate lawsuits so likely to fail also make them very important drivers of a necessary legal and public conversation. If the law is a living instrument, evolving together with the public consciousness, courts have the responsibility and competence to contribute to the legal process by providing an evolutive interpretation of the law. In this perspective, climate lawsuits offer a forum where the most controversial legal theories and imaginative strategies can be tested and discussed.

1   ADVANCING THE LEGAL CONVERSATION ON CLIMATE CHANGE

Climate lawsuits have recently challenged domestic courts with some quite challenging legal questions. Just to mention a few, in 2015, the Oslo district court was asked to take a stance on the extraterritoriality of Norway's human rights obligations.[6] The question was whether the government, in the exercise of power over its marine territory, namely when authorizing an oil excavation project, should have considered the consequences of its actions on the human rights of people living in other countries. In the same year, a Peruvian farmer sued Germany's largest electricity company (RWE) on the basis of its contribution to climate change. According to the claim, human emissions were responsible for the melting of the glaciers near the farmer's village of origin and for the consequential flooding of the lake located above it. Considering the application of different possible theories of causation, the plaintiffs asked RWE for the compensation of a portion of the costs that the

---

strategic cases (e.g. the enduring position of the power of perpetrators of massacres in the Guatemalan peace process, the 'war on terror' in the context of the resolution of land rights in Palestine under Israeli occupation).

5   *Fisher/Scotford/Barritt*, The Legally Disruptive Nature of Climate Change: Climate Change and Legal Disruption, The Modern Law Review 2017, 173.

6   Oslo District Court 4 January 2018, 16-166674TVI-OTIR/06, *Greenpeace Nordic Ass'n and Nature and Youth v. Ministry of Petroleum and Energy.*

village would have incurred to protect from flooding.[7] On the day of the 2019 global climate strike, Greta Thunberg and other young activists asked the UN Committee on the Right of the Child to declare that climate change is a children's rights issue and a matter of intergenerational equity.[8] In the meantime, other interesting questions have been directed to international and domestic fora around the world, referencing the present and imminent impacts of climate change.[9]

It is worth pointing out that the legal disruptiveness of those cases often makes courts reluctant to endorse courageous legal interpretations or even just to go into the merits of the case. However, as climate lawsuits increase in number and grow into a connected transnational movement, judges have the chance to make comparisons among them and eventually borrow foreign theories in their own jurisdictions. In this way, the social and political change hoped for could happen indirectly as a result of a dialogue between courts.

2   Boosting Public Awareness of Climate Change

Finally, even when claims fail in court, climate lawsuits can indirectly boost change by leading the conversation towards important aspects of the climate crisis. In a few cases, even when failing to recognize the parties' standing on rights-based claims, courts have acknowledged that climate change raises human rights obligations for governments[10] and that it represents an urgent problem.[11] As shown by sociolegal studies, this kind of statement has a high symbolic value in view of its potential to shift public perceptions on climate change.[12] Moreover, legal mobilization campaigns can have the effects of reframing climate change in ways that make it more relatable to the general public. In a recent article, Lisa Vanhala explained how an environmental organization in the USA managed, through a long legal campaign, to construct the idea of the polar bear as endangered by climate change.[13] Similarly, the Our Children Trust organization, along with other youth-led climate movements, might be successful in reframing climate change as a children's rights

---

7   Essen Regional Court 15 December 2016, 2 O 285/15, *Luciano Lliuya v. RWE AG.*
8   *Sacchi et al v. Argentina et al* (Committee on the Rights of the Child).
9   *Setzer/Brynes*, Global Trends in Climate Litigation 4. The global report indicates that claims seeking to hold corporate actors accountable for climate harms and challenging the states' failure to adapt to climate change represent an increasing trend in recent climate litigation.
10   Administrative Court of Berlin 31 October 2019, 10 K 412.18, *Family Farmers and Greenpeace Germany v. Germany.*
11   High Court of Ireland 19 September 2019, 793/2017, *Friends of the Irish Environment v. Ireland.*
12   *Peel/Osofsky*, Climate Change Litigation: Regulatory Pathways to Cleaner Energy (2015) 49 ff; *Rodríguez-Garavito*, Beyond the Courtroom: The Impact of Judicial Activism on Socioeconomic Rights in Latin America, Texas Law Review 2015/89, 1669.
13   *Vanhala*, Coproducing the Endangered Polar Bear: Science, Climate Change, and Legal Mobilization, Law & Policy 2020, 105.

issue, and, by doing so, appealing more strongly to the public imagination and consciousness.

3   CONCLUSION

To conclude, the global litigation movement, as well as the media focus on it, is proof that climate lawsuits have been able to not only engage legal scholars but also capture people's imagination. Here, it is worth pointing out that media attention will not automatically lead to social cohesion: the public debate on climate, even when on facts, is a likely source of social conflict. In fact, rights-based lawsuits confront industrialized states and their citizens with some of the most urgent moral questions for our generation. Among those, a prominent question is whether industrialized states are violating the rights of the children and of the populations in the Global South with their uninterrupted support to the fossil fuel industry. The climate activists hope that as the awareness about climate change and its sources grows and courts accept their role in opening the public conversation on climate change, the political representatives will feel compelled to remedy their inaction, or else, to answer those questions.

BIBLIOGRAPHY

Batros/Khan, Thinking Strategically about Climate Litigation, www.openglobal rights.org/thinking-strategically-about-climate-litigation/ (28 June 2020).

Duffy, Strategic Human Rights Litigation: Understanding and Maximising Impact (2018).

Fisher/Scotfort/Barritt, The Legally Disruptive Nature of Climate Change: Climate Change and Legal Disruption, The Modern Law Review 2017, 173.

Peel/Osofsky, A Rights Turn in Climate Change Litigation? Transnational Environmental Law 2018, 37.

Peel/Osofsky, Climate Change Litigation: Regulatory Pathways to Cleaner Energy (2015).

Rodríguez-Garavito, Beyond the Courtroom: The Impact of Judicial Activism on Socioeconomic Rights in Latin America, Texas Law Review 2015/89, 1669.

Setzer/Byrnes, Global Trends in Climate Litigation: A 2020 Snapshot, Policy Report (2020).

UN Environment/Columbia University, Sabin Center for Climate Change Law, The Status of Climate Change Litigation: A Global Review (2017).

Vanhala, Coproducing the Endangered Polar Bear: Science, Climate Change, and Legal Mobilization, Law & Policy 2020, 105.

Vanhala, Legal Opportunity Structure and the Paradox of Legal Mobilization by the Environmental Movement in the UK, Law & Society Review 2012/46, 523.

Wewerinke-Singh/Salili, Between Negotiations and Litigation: Vanuatu's Perspective on Loss and Damage from Climate Change, Climate Policy 2020, 681.

Wonneberger/Vliegenthart, Agenda-Setting Effects of Climate Change Litigation: Interrelations Across Issue Levels, Media, and Politics in the Case of Urgenda Against the Dutch Government, Environmental Communication 2012, 1.

Cases

Administrative Court of Berlin 31 October 2019, 10 K 412.18, *Family Farmers and Greenpeace Germany v. Germany*.

Essen Regional Court 15 December 2016, 2 O 285/15, *Luciano Lliuya v. RWE AG*.

High Court of Ireland 19 September 2019, 793/2017, *Friends of the Irish Environment v. Ireland*.

Oslo District Court 4 January 2018, 16-166674TVI-OTIR/06, *Greenpeace Nordic Ass'n and Nature and Youth v. Ministry of Petroleum and Energy*.

'Legitimate Expectations', State Subsidies and Climate Change Mitigation

Miriam Hofer

1 'Expectations' as a Legal Category

Heatwaves, droughts, floods – the consequences of climate change – are, as one might think, sufficiently well known today. However, there is no consensus on who should implement what mitigation measures, when and how. Studies reveal that people who deny the human influence on the climate can hardly be expected to change their lifestyles significantly for reasons of climate protection. Climate protection measures that directly affect the lives of individual citizens, such as speed limits on motorways and federal roads or higher electricity and heating costs, are particularly unpopular.[1]

At first sight, these expectations appear to be irrelevant from a legal point of view: the extent to which we assume that we will have to radically change our lifestyle in the coming years to mitigate climate change initially has political but hardly legal consequences. However, it gains legal relevance when our expectations enjoy legal protection, meaning their frustration leads to legal claims such as compensatory payments. This applies, in particular, to expectations safeguarded by the principle of protection of legitimate expectations.[2]

2 The Constitutional Dimension of State Subsidies and Incentives

In general, the principle of protection of legitimate expectations applies, inter alia, in the context of state measures with adverse consequences for the individual if their effects were not foreseeable. According to the well-established case law of the Austrian constitutional court, legitimate expectations are protected in such a way that disproportionate, sudden

---

[1] *See, e.g., Seidl*, Ökosteuern sind unbeliebt und wären nur in Wien mehrheitsfähig, www.derstandard.at/story/2000114843868/oekosteuern-sind-unbeliebt-und-waeren-nur-in-wien-mehrheitsfaehig (22 February 2020).

[2] For Austria, such legal protection arises i.e. from Art 7 B-VG (Federal Constitutional Law, available in English at www.ris.bka.gv.at/Dokument.wxe?Abfrage=Erv&Dokumentnummer=ERV_1930_1).

and surprising infringements of legal positions, the existence of which could be relied on for good reasons, are unconstitutional.[3]

This is the case if the state explicitly induces citizens to make certain dispositions through specific legal incentives or state subsidies, whose advantages it then denies. In this context, the Austrian constitutional court declared the extension of a night driving ban to low-noise lorries to be unconstitutional. Shortly before that, a night driving ban on lorries had been enacted, explicitly excluding low-noise lorries and thus inducing many haulers to invest in low-noise lorries.[4]

Of course, in general, an infringement of a legal position can be objectively well founded and thus justified, especially for reasons of climate protection.[5] However, suppose the state deliberately and specifically promotes GHG-intensive behaviour despite its obligation to reduce emissions. Subsequently it restricts this behaviour in order to meet its emission reduction targets under EU and international law. Such interference can probably not be considered justified.

3 Social Transformation and Legal Continuity

The goals of the Paris Agreement,[6] the EU's climate targets[7] and the predicted consequences of exceeding the target of 1.5°C/2°C reveal that a comprehensive societal and economic transition towards a carbon-neutral society is inevitable and will require measures that affect everyone's lives. Effective mitigation measures should be adopted today rather than tomorrow to protect the climate and ensure legal certainty and legal continuity – long transition periods, resulting from a ban on oil-fired heating and coal-fired power plants, are unavoidable under constitutional law anyway. A ban on oil heating systems in Austria, for example, shall provide a staged phase-out of oil by 2025 (older oil heating systems) and 2035 (!) for newer oil heating systems.[8]

---

3   *Holoubek* in *Korinek/Holoubek/Bezemek/Fuchs/Martin/Zellenberg* (eds), Österreichisches Bundesverfas-sungsrecht (16.EL 2021) Art. 7 B-VG Rz 363 ff. For EU law *see also*, *e.g.*, ECJ C-5/16, *Poland v. European Parliament and Council of the European Union*, ECLI:EU:C:2018:483.

4   VfSlg 12.944/1991.

5   *See, e.g.*, ECJ C-5/16, ECLI:EU:C:2018:483, Rz 112.

6   Art. 2 Z 1 lit a Paris Agreement, available at https://unfccc.int/sites/default/files/english_paris_agreement.pdf.

7   *EU Member States*, Update of the NDC of the European Union and its Member States, https://www4.unfccc.int/sites/ndcstaging/PublishedDocuments/European%20Union%20First/EU_NDC_Submission_December%202020.pdf (17 December 2020).

8   *See ORF*, Bund und Länder einig: Heizen künftig ohne Öl, Gas und Kohle, https://orf.at/stories/3209796/ (19 April 2021).

4   CLIMATE-DAMAGING STATE SUBSIDIES IN THE CORONA CRISIS

Special attention regarding the creation of legitimate expectation should be drawn to state subsidies and financial incentives in the context of the corona crisis. For example, a scrappage or purchase premium, as was discussed for the purchase of new (low-emission) petrol and diesel vehicles in Germany,[9] would create such legally relevant legitimate expectations and narrow the scope of the state in its climate mitigation policy: if the state actively promotes the purchase of a new vehicle with a conventional combustion engine by granting financial incentives in the form of state premiums, it creates an individual expectation that purchasers will also be allowed to use their vehicle in the coming years. Driving bans or legal restrictions on the use of cars with conventional combustion engines would thus be ruled out until at least 2030 (assuming a minimum period of use of 8 years, which is the assumption of Austrian tax law, and a premium granted in 2021).[10]

If, for that reason, climate targets could not be met, this would result in massive financial consequences, owing to the necessity of certificate purchases. At the same time, however, implementing corresponding measures in the transport sector that frustrate legitimate expectations would also lead to severe financial consequences, in the form of necessary compensatory payments for the owners of cars with conventional combustion engines.[11] State subsidies to tackle the corona crisis should therefore be designed to be as climate friendly as possible, or at least climate neutral: expectations that climate-damaging behaviour will continue to be possible in the future without any legal hurdles should under no circumstances be supported by the state, despite the threat of an economic crisis.

BIBLIOGRAPHY

EU Member States, Update of the NDC of the European Union and Its Member States, https://www4.unfccc.int/sites/ndcstaging/PublishedDocuments/European%20Union%20 First/EU_NDC_Submission_December%202020.pdf (17 December 2020).

Holoubek in *Korinek/Holoubek/Bezemek/Fuchs/Martin/Zellenberg* (eds), Österreichisches Bundesverfassungsrecht (16.EL 2021) Art 7 B-VG.

Öhlinger/Eberhard, Verfassungsrecht[12] (2019).

---

9   ZDF, Neue Forderungen: Kommt die Kaufprämie?, www.zdf.de/nachrichten/wirtschaft/coronavirus-auto-kaufpraemie-100.html (27 May 2020).
10   § 8 Abs 6 Z 1 Einkommensteuergesetz 1988 (EStG) BGBl 1988/400 idF BGBl I 2021/71.
11   *Öhlinger/Eberhard*, Verfassungsrecht[12] (2019) 407 f.

ORF, Bund und Länder einig: Heizen künftig ohne Öl, Gas und Kohle, https://orf.at/stories/ 3209796/ (19 April 2021).

Seidl, Ökosteuern sind unbeliebt und wären nur in Wien mehrheitsfähig, www.derstandard.at/story/2000114843868/oekosteuern-sind-unbeliebt-und-waeren-nur-in-wien-mehrheitsfaehig (22 February 2020).

ZDF, Neue Forderungen: Kommt die Kaufprämie?, www.zdf.de/nachrichten/wirtschaft/ coronavirus-auto-kaufpraemie-100.html (27 May 2020).

CASES

ECJ C-5/16, *Poland v. European Parliament and Council of the European Union*, ECLI:EU:C:2018:483.

VfSlg 12.944/1991.

WTO Rules on Border Carbon Adjustment for the EU ETS: Key GATT Principles

Lydia A. Omuko-Jung[*]

1 Introduction

In order to reduce the risk of carbon leakage and ensure the competitiveness of EU companies subject to the EU Emissions Trading System (EU ETS), the European Commission plans to propose a carbon border adjustment mechanism (CBAM). In its communication on the European Green Deal, the Commission noted that *should differences in levels of ambition worldwide persist, as the EU increases its climate ambition, the Commission will propose a carbon border adjustment mechanism, for selected sectors, to reduce the risk of carbon leakage.*[1] In fact, the Commission hopes to raise €5 billion to €14 billion per year from the CBAM to finance its post-COVID recovery budget.[2]

A carbon border adjustment is basically a tariff on imports from countries without comparable climate policies to ensure that importers face the same costs of emissions as domestic producers.[3] For instance, country X levies a carbon tax on domestic producers or has an emission trading scheme. To ensure that domestic producers are not disadvantaged against imports, country X would levy an equivalent tax on imports from countries that do not have comparably stringent climate policies. Additionally, to ensure that domestic products are competitive in the global market, exporters from country X may be eligible for rebates for the tax paid.

This is not the first time that it has been proposed in the EU. In 2007, the Commission, in an unpublished draft that sought to amend the EU ETS proposed a 'Future Allowance Import Requirement', which sought to apply a border carbon adjustment to products

[*] This work is funded by the Austrian Science Fund (FWF) under Research Grant W1256 (Doctoral Programme Climate Change: Uncertainties, Thresholds and Coping Strategies).

[1] Communication from the Commission to the European Parliament, the European Council, the Council, the European Economic and Social Committee and the Committee of the Regions, The European Green Deal, COM (2019) 640 final of 11 December 2019.

[2] *European Commission and Directorate-General for the Budget*, Financing the Recovery Plan for Europe, https://op.europa.eu/publication/manifestation_identifier/PUB_KV0220280ENN (last accessed 8 June 2021).

[3] *Hufbauer/Charnovits/Kim*, Global Warming and the World Trading System (2009); *Mehling/Van Asselt et al*, Designing Border Carbon Adjustments for Enhanced Climate Action, American Journal of International Law 2019/113, 433.

exposed to the risk of carbon leakage.[4] The second and third proposals were by the French government – one in 2009 and another in 2016 – which sought to include importers in the EU ETS.[5] All these proposals did not sail through, and one of the fears has been violation of World Trade Organisation (WTO) rules.

In the most recent proposal, the Commission has indicated that the proposed measure will comply with WTO rules and other international obligations of the EU.[6] Members of European Parliament (MEP) have also signalled that that they would like to see a WTO-compliant CBAM.[7] The question is, can the EU make its imports greener while respecting the WTO rules? Is it possible to design a WTO-compatible carbon border adjustment? This article provides some design features considered necessary for a WTO-compliant CBAM.

2   WTO Principles on Border Carbon Adjustments

The question of whether the CBAM will be WTO compliant depends substantially on the design of the mechanism and how it will be implemented. While the Commission has not released the proposed design, which is expected in July 2021, the following proposals were canvassed in the Commission's public consultation:[8]

a. A tariff on imports at the EU border on selected products whose production is in sectors that are at risk of carbon leakage.

b. Extending the EU ETS to imports, requiring emission allowances under the EU ETS by either foreign producers or importers.

c. The obligation to purchase allowances from a specific pool outside the EU ETS dedicated to imports, which would mirror the ETS price.

d. Carbon tax on consumption of selected products whose production is in sectors that are at risk of carbon leakage, applied on imports and EU production.

---

4   Proposal for a Directive of the European Parliament and of the Council amending Directive 2003/87/EC to enhance cost-effective emission reductions and low-carbon investments, COM (2015) 337 final of 15 July 2015.

5   *Mehling/Van Asselt et al*, Designing Border Carbon Adjustments 450-451.

6   COM (2019) 640 final, 5.

7   Resolution (EU) 2020/2043 of the European parliament of 10 March 2021 towards a WTO-Compatible EU Carbon Border Adjustment Mechanism, P9_TA(2021)0071, para 7, www.europarl.europa.eu/doceo/document/TA-9-2021-0071_EN.pdf (last accessed 7 June 2021).

8   European Commission, Summary Report on Public Consultation on the Carbon Border Adjustment Mechanism (CBAM), https://ec.europa.eu/info/law/better-regulation/have-your-say/initiatives/12228-Carbon-Border-Adjustment-Mechanism/public-consultation_en (last accessed 9 June 2021).

The fourth option, however, raises some challenge, as it would involve passing of an EU-wide carbon tax, which requires unanimous backing by all EU Member States.[9] Previous attempts by the European Commission to introduce EU-wide carbon have not been successful,[10] which would make this the most unfavourable option. There have also been indications that the EU is likely to go for the third option. In the resolution passed by the European parliament, the MEP opined that importers should buy allowances from a separate pool to the EU ETS.[11] There have also been suggestions, based on leaked documents, that the Commission's proposal will take the form of the third option, where a CBAM Authority will sell CBAM certificates based on a calculation linked to the prices under the EU ETS.[12] The Commission has, however, indicated that the work on CBAM proposals is still ongoing and that no final decision has been taken on design proposals.[13] Whichever form it takes, the design needs to comply with the WTO rules.

2.1   Non-discrimination Principle Under GATT[14]

One of the fundamental principles under WTO is *non-discrimination*, which requires:
a. any advantage granted to imports of one member to be unconditionally granted to *like* products of all the other members (Most Favoured Nation (MFN));[15]
b. imports not to be treated any less favourably than *like* domestic products (national treatment).[16]

---

9   Consolidated Version of the Treaty on the Functioning of the European Union 2012 paras. 192 and 113 require legislation of primarily fiscal nature and rules on indirect taxation to be enacted unanimously by the council in accordance with a special legislative procedure. While there is uncertainty on the interpretation of 'primarily fiscal nature', such taxes are believed to require unanimity of council. *See* Advocate General's opinion in ECJ C-36/98, *Spain v. Council of the European Union*, ECLI:EU:C:2000:246; *Weishaar*, Carbon Taxes at EU Level: Introduction Issues and Barriers, WIFO Working Papers 2018/556, 2, http://hdl.handle.net/10419/179310 (last accessed 9 June 2021).
10   *Weishaar*, Carbon Taxes at EU Level 8.
11   Resolution (EU) 2020/2043 para. 16.
12   *Taylor*, LEAK: EU's Carbon Border Tariff to Target Steel, Cement, Power, www.euractiv.com/section/energy-environment/news/eus-carbon-border-tariff-to-target-steel-cement-power/ (last accessed 8 June 2021); *Watson*, EU Carbon Border Mechanism to Require Surrender of Certificates: Draft Proposal, www.spglobal.com/platts/en/market-insights/latest-news/electric-power/060421-eu-carbon-border-mechanism-to-require-surrender-of-certificates-draft-proposal (4 June 2021).
13   *Watson*, EU Carbon Border Mechanism.
14   General Agreement on Tariffs and Trade, 30 October 1947, 61 Stat. A-11, 55 UNTS 194, as incorporated in General Agreement on Tariffs and Trade 1994, Marrakesh Agreement Establishing the World Trade Organization 1994 (1867 UNTS 187).
15   Art. I GATT 1994.
16   Art. III GATT 1994.

The first thing is that the CBAM should not favour domestic production over imports. This means that if a border carbon tax is imposed on imported cement, importers should pay a tax equivalent to the permit price had the cement been domestically produced. If the CBAM takes the form of permit purchase, then importers would be required to buy emission allowance at the same price and conditions as those applicable to purchases of like products made by domestic producers. A similar amount of emission allowances should be available and accessible in the market to both importers and domestic producers.

For compliance with this principle, auctioning of allowances needs to be a prerequisite rather than free allocation. The EU will need to do away with free allowances if CBAM extends the EU ETS to imports. Maintaining free allowances would mean that domestic producers enjoy favourable treatment as they do not have to pay a carbon price, while an importer is obliged to pay. If free allowances are maintained, the CBAM should be imposed only on the share of emissions embedded in imported goods that exceeds the benchmark for free allocation.[17] This makes the importer liable only for that portion of emissions of which domestic producers do not benefit from the free allocation.

The fluctuating carbon prices in the EU ETS may lead to violation of the non-discrimination principle where the CBAM takes the form of a carbon tax. Consequently, a price floor can be implemented within the EU ETS, which could then be used to determine the tax rate.[18] This ensures that the permit price would never go below the tax paid by importers for like products.

Secondly, importers with products from different countries should access the emission allowances (or pay taxes) under the same conditions and prices. There should be no exemption or preferential treatment of products from any third-party Member States, except products from least developed countries, which can receive some favourable treatment or exemption.[19] Thus, providing preferential treatment on the basis of comparable or ambitious climate policies of the country of origin could bring CBAM in conflict with Article I GATT. Rather, producers should be able to show that they have adopted low-carbon production methods or that they have already paid a carbon price in respect of the products.

Determining the carbon content of products to base the adjustment level could also raise discrimination issues. It is still unclear whether, for instance, high-carbon and

---

17   *Marcu/Mehling/Cosbey*, CBAM for the EU: A Policy Proposal, European Roundtable on Climate Change and Sustainable Transition (ERCST), https://ercst.org/border-carbon-adjustments-in-the-eu/ (last accessed 7 June 2021).

18   *Krenek/Sommer/Schratzenstaller*, A WTO-Compatible Border Tax Adjustment for the ETS to Finance the EU Budget, WIFO Working Papers 2020/596, 14. Available at www.wifo.ac.at/jart/prj3/wifo/resources/person_dokument/person_dokument.jart?publikationsid=65841&mime_type=application/pdf (last accessed 7 June 2021).

19   Decision on Differential and More Favourable Treatment, Reciprocity and Fuller Participation of Developing Countries [1979] BISD 26S/203.

low-carbon content steel would be considered as *like* products. If considered like, then an adjustment level based on carbon content of products would amount to discrimination not only between imported and like domestic products but also between imports from different countries. To avoid this possibility (and also for administrative purposes), the adjustment could be based on a predetermined benchmark, which could be EU's average emissions intensity. Importers with better performance than the benchmark could, however, be granted an opportunity to show the actual carbon content of their products (through a verifiable process) so that the adjustment is based on the carbon content of their products.

2.2   Exceptions Under Article XX GATT

Where the CBAM violates the non-discrimination principle, it may be justified under the exceptions in Article XX GATT if it can be shown that it is *necessary to protect human, animal or plant life or health* or that it *relates to the conservation of exhaustible natural resources*.[20] The environmental effectiveness of a measure is a relevant consideration for this. For CBAM to pass, the EU needs to demonstrate that the goal of CBAM is to preserve the climate. A CBAM designed to reduce emissions and that actually makes a material contribution in emission reduction would be justifiable. However, if the effect of the CBAM is that reductions in some sectors are replaced by increased emissions in, for instance, export sectors, then it may not comply with the exception. Additionally, targeting carbon-intensive products at significant risk of carbon leakage makes it easier to justify the environmental effectiveness of the CBAM. The Commission already hinted that the proposed CBAM would be introduced in selected sectors that are at risk of carbon leakage.[21] This not only strengthens its legal defensibility under WTO but also limits the administrative burden, considering that the administrative burden of CBAM increases proportionally to the number of sectors to which it is applied.[22]

Secondly, the CBAM should *not be applied in a manner that would constitute a means of arbitrary or unjustifiable discrimination between countries where the same conditions prevail*.[23] The EU will have to demonstrate that the proposed CBAM adjusts only for the internal level of carbon pricing and is not in fact designed to increase EU industries' relative competitiveness. Another way to demonstrate compliance with this provision is for the EU to take steps to negotiate with countries likely to be affected by the CBAM.[24]

---

20   Art. XX (b) and (g) GATT 1994.
21   COM (2019) 640 final, 5.
22   *Monjon/Quirion*, How to Design a Border Adjustment for the European Union Emissions Trading System? Energy Policy 2010/38, 5199 (5205).
23   Para. XX GATT 1994 (introductory paragraph).
24   United States – Import Prohibition of Certain Shrimp and Shrimp Products – Report of the Appellate Body [1998] WT/DS58/AB/R [166].

Additionally, the CBAM could be designed with flexibility to take into account conditions in exporting countries.[25] This is because discrimination could also occur where a measure fails to take into account the different conditions in different countries. Thus, CBAM with preferential treatment of least developed countries would not only gain the support of this provision (and comply with MFN exemptions) but also support the common but differentiated responsibilities principle under the Paris Agreement.

3 CONCLUSION

Considering the political, legal and practical challenges, as well the current political discussions, the CBAM is likely to take the form of extending the EU ETS to imports by requiring importers to purchase emissions allowances under the EU ETS or from a specific pool dedicated to imports. To ensure compliance with international trade law, the EU needs to do away with free allowances so that importers can access them on similar conditions as domestic producers. If free allowances are maintained, CBAM should be imposed only on the share of emissions embedded in imports that exceeds the benchmark for free allocation. More importantly, differentiation should be based on the emission intensity or already paid carbon price for the specific products as opposed to being country specific. However, least developed countries can be exempted or granted preferential treatment. Considering the administrative complexity and environmental effectiveness, it is better to limit the scope of CBAM to carbon-intensive and trade-sensitive sectors.

BIBLIOGRAPHY

Communication from the Commission to the European Parliament, the European Council, the Council, the European Economic and Social Committee and the Committee of the Regions, The European Green Deal, COM (2019) 640 final of 11 December 2019.

Consolidated Version of the Treaty on the Functioning of the European Union 2012.

Decision on Differential and More Favourable Treatment, Reciprocity and Fuller Participation of Developing Countries [1979] BISD 26S/203.

ECJ C-36/98, *Spain v. Council of the European Union*, ECLI:EU:C:2000:246.

---

25   US Shrimp Para. 165.

European Commission and Directorate-General for the Budget, Financing the Recovery Plan for Europe, https://op.europa.eu/publication/manifestation_identifier/PUB_KV0220280ENN (last accessed 8 June 2021).

European Commission, Summary Report on Public Consultation on the Carbon Border Adjustment Mechanism (CBAM), https://ec.europa.eu/info/law/better-regulation/have-your-say/initiatives/12228-Carbon-Border-Adjustment-Mechanism/public-consultation_en (last accessed 9 June 2021).

General Agreement on Tariffs and Trade, 30 October 1947, 61 Stat. A-11, 55 UNTS 194, as incorporated in General Agreement on Tariffs and Trade 1994, Marrakesh Agreement Establishing the World Trade Organization 1994 (1867 UNTS 187).

Hufbauer/Charnovits/Kim, Global Warming and the World Trading System (2009).

Krenek/Sommer/Schratzenstaller, A WTO-Compatible Border Tax Adjustment for the ETS to Finance the EU Budget, WIFO Working Papers 2020/596, 14, www.wifo.ac.at/jart/prj3/wifo/resources/person_dokument/person_dokument.jart?publikationsid=65841&mime_type=application/pdf (last accessed 7 June 2021).

Marcu/Mehling/Cosbey, CBAM for the EU: A Policy Proposal, European Roundtable on Climate Change and Sustainable Transition (ERCST), https://ercst.org/border-carbon-adjustments-in-the-eu/ (last accessed 7 June 2021).

Mehling/Van Asselt et al, Designing Border Carbon Adjustments for Enhanced Climate Action, American Journal of International Law 2019/113, 433.

Monjon/Quirion, How to Design a Border Adjustment for the European Union Emissions Trading System? Energy Policy 2010/38, 5199 (5205).

Proposal for a Directive of the European Parliament and of the Council amending Directive 2003/87/EC to enhance cost-effective emission reductions and low-carbon investments, COM (2015) 337 final of 15 July 2015.

Resolution (EU) 2020/2043 of the European Parliament of 10 March 2021 towards a WTO-Compatible EU Carbon Border Adjustment Mechanism, P9_TA(2021)0071, para 7, www.europarl.europa.eu/doceo/document/TA-9-2021-0071_EN.pdf (last accessed 7 June 2021).

Taylor, LEAK: EU's Carbon Border Tariff to Target Steel, Cement, Power, www.euractiv.com/section/energy-environment/news/eus-carbon-border-tariff-to-target-steel-cement-power/ (last accessed 8 June 2021).

United States – Import Prohibition of Certain Shrimp and Shrimp Products – Report of the Appellate Body [1998] WT/DS58/AB/R [166].

Watson, EU Carbon Border Mechanism to Require Surrender of Certificates: Draft Proposal, www.spglobal.com/platts/en/market-insights/latest-news/electric-power/060421-eu-carbon-border-mechanism-to-require-surrender-of-certificates-draft-proposal (4 June 2021).

Weishaar, Carbon Taxes at EU Level: Introduction Issues and Barriers, WIFO Working Papers 2018/556, 2, http://hdl.handle.net/10419/179310 (last accessed 9 June 2021).

Balancing Decisions in Climate Law

How Economic Instruments Could Help to Increase Their Acceptance

Christoph Romirer

1 Weighing of Interests: An Environmental Law Instrument

Hardly any area of Austrian public law is free of balancing decisions.[1] Opposing interests clash at all levels of the legal system and require careful consideration by the legally authorized decision-making body. Provisions with balancing implications are also frequently found in matters of environmental law:[2] For instance, the public interest in the realization of a project regularly conflicts with the public interest in the preservation of surface water quality or natural ecosystems. The instrument of balancing interests is particularly present in nature conservation law, as it provides a variety of obligations to protect nature and landscape and, consequently, prohibits interference that could negatively impact them, but, on the other hand, contains few 'hard' or irrevocable stipulations which cannot be bypassed with a balancing decision.[3] A recent study on the province of Vorarlberg's nature conservation law[4] shows that this system, following the administrative case-by-case practice,[5] raises concerns from an ecological point of view: Even though the majority of projects to be realized bears negative impacts on nature and landscape, only little applications get rejected. Environmental goods, however, are exhaustible resources.

---

1   *See Lienbacher*, Abwägungsentscheidungen im öffentlichen Recht, in Khakzadeh-Leiler/Schmid/Weber (eds), Interessenabwägung und Abwägungsentscheidungen, Forschungen aus Staat und Recht, Volume 175 (2014) 85.

2   *E.g.* § 27 para. 3 StNSchG 2017, § 17 para. 5 UVP-G 2000, § 4 para. 3 in conjunction with para. 1 BStG 1971, § 71 para. 1 lit. d LFG.

3   *See* § 23 para. 1 Vbg GNL.

4   *Schulev-Steindl/Romirer*, Interessenabwägung im Vorarlberger Naturschutzrecht – Funktionen, Dimensionen und Evaluierung (2019), www.naturschutzrat.at/studien/; also *see Schulev-Steindl/Romirer*, Interessenabwägung im Naturschutzrecht – Ein Problemaufriss am Beispiel Vorarlbergs, RdU 2020, 187.

5   It is in the nature of the administrative procedure to decide on a case-by-case basis. From the point of view of environmental protection, this is not without problems, since many individual – and legitimate – permits can have a major impact on the overall quality of our natural resources.

2   CLIMATE PROTECTION AND/OR ECONOMIC GROWTH?

As the appeal procedure for the construction of a third runway at Vienna International Airport showed, the process of balancing and resolving interest conflicts holds considerable potential for controversy. Accordingly, a major stir was caused when the Austrian Federal Administrative Court (BVwG) reversed the decision of the Environmental Impact Assessment (EIA) authority, thus revoking the Flughafen Wien AG's permit. The court reasoned that the public interest in reducing GHG emissions in Austria, complying with EU and national climate law obligations, would outweigh the public interest in realizing the project.[6] A lively media, social, and legal debate followed, as the BVwG's decision was – internationally – the very first where a project's approval had been repealed on account of climate protection. However, shortly afterwards, the Austrian Constitutional Court (VfGH) overturned the Federal Administrative Court's decision – no less controversially – on the grounds that it had carried out the weighing process erroneously and acted arbitrarily.[7] The legal dispute continued for two more years, but in the end, the third runway may rightfully be constructed.[8] Cases like this put the basic principles of environmental proceedings as well as the system of administrative jurisdiction to test and reveal and emphasize the political dimension of environmental and climate law.[9]

The main problem is that balancing opposing interests – be they economical and ecological, as in the Vienna Airport case, or of different ecological nature only (typically occurring in approval procedures for renewable energy projects[10]) – can be justified in a

---

6   BVwG 2 February 2017, W109 2000179-1; also *see Kirchengast/Madner/Schulev-Steindl/Steininger/Hollaus/Karl*, Flughafen Wien: Untersagung der dritten Piste durch das BVwG, RdU 2017,121.

7   VfGH 29 June 2017, E 875/2017, E 886/2017; critical comments in *Fuchs*, Interessenabwägung, Ermessen, dritte Piste Flughafen Wien. Anmerkungen zu VfGH 29 June 2017, E 875/2017, E 886/2017 und BVwG 2 February 2017, W109 2000179-1/291E, ÖJZ 2017, 192; *Hollaus*, Austrian Constitutional Court: Considering Climate Change as a Public Interest is Arbitrary – Refusal of Third Runway Permit Annulled, ICL Journal 2017, 467 (https://doi.org/10.1515/icl-2017-0070); *Madner/Schulev-Steindl*, Dritte Piste – Klimaschutz als Willkür? Anmerkungen zu VfGH 29 June 2017, E 875/2017, E 886/2017, ZÖR 2017, 589; *Merli*, Ein seltsamer Fall von Willkür: Die VfGH-Entscheidung zur dritten Piste des Flughafens Wien, wbl 2017, 682; *Wagner*, Was bislang geschah: Staatszieldebatte/VfGH hebt Urteil Dritte Piste auf, RdU 2017, 149; supporting the view of the VfGH *Niederhuber*, Dritte-Piste-Entscheidung zeigt: Es gilt das Gesetz, DerStandard 2017/36/01; *Schmelz*, Der VfGH zur dritten Piste - Klimaschutz im Widerspruch zu Rechtsstaat und Demokratie?, ZGV 2017, 288.

8   VwGH 6 March 2019, Ro 2017/03/0031; also see *Kirchengast/Madner/Schulev-Steindl/Steininger/Hollaus/Karl*, VwGH zur "Dritten Piste": "Cruise-Emissionen" im UVP-Verfahren trotz Relevanz des Klimaschutzes nicht zurechenbar, RdU 2020, 72.

9   In that sense *Bergthaler*, Die "dritte Piste" im zweiten Rechtsgang oder: Das Gebot der CO_2-Neutralität, in Baumgartner (eds), Jahrbuch Öffentliches Recht 2018 (2018), 176.

10   *Dulluri/Rat*, The Green-Green Dilemma – Reconciling the Conflict Between Renewable Energy and Biodiversity, The Journal of Health, Environment & Education, Vol 11, 2019, 6 (https://doi.org/10.18455/19002); also see *Geringer/Romirer*, Klima- und Naturschutzrecht im ökologischen Zielkonflikt: Zur Interessenab-

legally comprehensible way, but not in a logically compelling form.[11] For the different interests to be taken into account, there are *de facto* no comparable evaluation standards and no generally valid comparison mechanisms or criteria. Does the expansion of a ski area bring more benefits for the common good than, for example, the preservation of the landscape that would be potentially affected by it?[12] Is a new bike path in the woods or a natural forest area worth more?[13] What about the preservation of a natural surface water body's quality in comparison to the construction of a hydroelectric power plant for "green" power – which is of greater importance?[14] How much does a stable climate save public finances? What's the 'cost' of a state's inertness with regard to its possibilities to undertake climate protection measures?[15]

As illustrated, the decision made at the end of a weighing process is always one of several alternatives for which the supposedly better arguments speak. Owing to its unavoidable subjectivity, such a "value decision" is ultimately associated with a slight degree of irrationality.[16] According to the Austrian Administrative Court (VwGH), the legal conformity of such decisions is to be measured by whether the respective grounds are outlined as comprehensively, precisely, and transparently as possible and whether the competing interests are balanced in accordance with the laws of reasoning, principles of experience and, if applicable, scientific findings.[17] However, scientific findings cannot be provided by the legal system alone – fortunately, economic instruments could very well help to bring more clarity.

3   MONETARIZING ECOLOGICAL INTERESTS

Environmental economics is familiar with the concept of 'public goods', which are non-rival and non-excludable per definition.[18] Using the example of climate protection not only as an environmental but also as an economic 'good' to be preserved, these characteristics are

---

wägung in der Energiewende, in Ennöckl/Niederhuber (eds), Umweltrecht. Jahrbuch 2019, 246; *Gärditz*, Ökologische Binnenkonflikte im Klimaschutzrecht, DVBl 2010, 214.

11 *See Uerpmann*, Das öffentliche Interesse (1999) 286.

12 *E.g.* § 6 lit c, e in conjunction with § 29 para. 1 lit b TNSchG 2005.

13 § 17 ForstG.

14 § 104a Abs 2 WRG.

15 For the case of Austria, only *see Steininger*, Die gesamtwirtschaftlichen Folgekosten des klimapolitischen Nicht-Handelns am Beispiel Österreich, in Kirchengast/Schulev-Steindl/Schnedl (eds), Klimaschutzrecht zwischen Wunsch und Wirklichkeit (2018) 33.

16 *Uerpmann*, Interesse, 284, 286, 288 f with further references.

17 *E.g.* VwGH 9 June 2020, Ra 2019/10/0075; VwGH 16 December 2019, Ra 2018/03/0066; VwGH 9 November 2016, Ro 2014/10/0044; VwGH 18 February 2015, 2013/10/0074; VwGH 24 January 2013, 2011/07/0252; VwGH 2 January 2010, 2008/07/0033; VwGH 02 October 2007, 2004/10/0174.

18 *Perman et al*, Natural Resource and Environmental Economics[4] (2011) 113 f.

more or less perfectly met: a stable climate can be consumed by everyone, while the negative consequences of climate change will affect each person and society as a whole as well.[19] In other words, although the preservation of the climate undoubtedly has some (non-use[20]) value, its use does not entail any costs for individuals.[21] This leads to a situation where, in the case of individually rational behaviour, climate protection and other public goods are not sufficiently provided or not provided at all. This represents a typical market failure caused by positive and negative externalities,[22] which must be compensated by legislation or else by administration.

Interests that run counter to the preservation of environmental goods are typically quantifiable – and actually must be, as applicants are required to adequately outline the (typically economic) benefits of their project before the granting authority. The value of nature, water, or other 'green' assets, however, is more difficult to specify. If climate protection could be assessed in monetary terms – for instance, by identifying its true societal value – the lack of comparability could be minimized, and, consequently, the comprehensibility and acceptance of weighing decisions could be increased. In this context, economic instruments valuing environmental goods[23] appear to be quite promising, calculating the willingness to pay for climate protection measures and the willingness to accept deterioration due to the non-implementation of such measures.[24] The objective it to determine the total economic value[25] of such a good, distinguishing between use-dependent and use-independent individual preferences. Methods such as the contingent valuation approach serve to integrate society as such into the balancing process, to reveal its preferences with regard to certain climate harming projects and to convert these into monetary values.

In an economic sense, a proper balancing decision would entail more benefits than costs for society, revealing the "true" value of climate protection in relation to the value of a certain project with negative impacts on it. Subsequently, the decision would also be

---

19   *Cf Sturm/Vogt*, Umweltökonomik. Eine anwendungsorientierte Einführung (2011) 49 f.

20   More in *Bastien-Olvera/Moore*, Use and Non-use Value of Nature and the Social Cost of Carbon, Nature Sustainability, Vol 4, 2021, 101 (https://doi.org/10.1038/s41893-020-00615-0); *Hutchinson/Chilton/Davies*, Measuring Non-use Value of Environmental Goods Using the Contingent Valuation Method: Problems of Information and Cognition and the Application of Cognitive Questionnaire Design Methods, Journal of Agricultural Economics, Vol 46, 1995, 97 (https://doi.org/10.1111/j.1477-9552.1995.tb00755.x).

21   Also known as the economic issue of a 'free rider problem'.

22   *Perman et al* 121 ff.

23   On this topic see *Kontoleon/Macrory/Swanson*, Individual Preference-based Values and Environmental Decision Making: Should Valuation Have Its Day in Court? Research in Law and Economics, Vol 20, 2020, 179.

24   See *Hanemann*, Willingness to Pay and Willingness to Accept: How Much Can They Differ?, in The American Economic Review, Vol 81 (3), 1991, 635.

25   *Perman et al* 413 f.

legitimized legally, as any kind of subjectivity/irrationality would have been removed. Consequently, increased societal acceptance must follow.

Summary: Balancing decisions reveal the limitations of law, as it is not possible to assign a distinct value to environmental goods like climate protection with legal means. Economic instruments, however, may help to overcome these obstacles by monetarizing climate protection, creating a basis on which the opposing interests can be compared objectively, thus rendering balancing decisions comprehensible.

Bibliography

Bastien-Olvera/Moore, Use and Non-use Value of Nature and the Social Cost of Carbon, Nature Sustainability, Vol 4, 2021 (https://doi.org/10.1038/s41893-020-00615-0).

Bergthaler, Die "dritte Piste" im zweiten Rechtsgang oder: Das Gebot der CO2-Neutralität, in *Baumgartner* (ed), Jahrbuch Öffentliches Recht 2018 (2018), 176.

Dulluri/Rat, The Green-Green Dilemma – Reconciling the Conflict Between Renewable Energy and Biodiversity, The Journal of Health, Environment & Education, Vol 11, 2019, 6 (https://doi.org/10.18455/19002).

Fuchs, Interessenabwägung, Ermessen, dritte Piste Flughafen Wien. Anmerkungen zu VfGH 29 June 2017, E 875/2017, E 886/2017 und BVwG 2 February 2017, W109 2000179-1/291E, ÖJZ 2017, 192.

Gärditz, Ökologische Binnenkonflikte im Klimaschutzrecht, DVBl 2010, 214.

Geringer/Romirer, Klima- und Naturschutzrecht im ökologischen Zielkonflikt: Zur Interessenabwägung in der Energiewende, in *Ennöckl/Niederhuber* (eds), Umweltrecht. Jahrbuch 2019, 246.

Hanemann, Willingness to Pay and Willingness to Accept: How Much Can They Differ? The American Economic Review, Vol 81 (3), 1991, 635.

Hollaus, Austrian Constitutional Court: Considering Climate Change as a Public Interest is Arbitrary – Refusal of Third Runway Permit Annulled, ICL Journal 2017, 467 (https://doi.org/10.1515/icl-2017-0070).

Hutchinson/Chilton/Davies, Measuring Non-use Value of Environmental Goods Using the Contingent Valuation Method: Problems of Information and Cognition and the Application of Cognitive Questionnaire Design Methods, Journal of Agricultural Economics, Vol 46, 1995, 97 (https://doi.org/10.1111/j.1477-9552.1995.tb00755.x).

Kirchengast/Madner/Schulev-Steindl/Steininger/Hollaus/Karl, Flughafen Wien: Untersagung der dritten Piste durch das BVwG, RdU 2017, 121.

Kirchengast/Madner/Schulev-Steindl/Steininger/Hollaus/Karl, VwGH zur "Dritten Piste": "Cruise-Emissionen" im UVP-Verfahren trotz Relevanz des Klimaschutzes nicht zurechenbar, RdU 2020, 72.

Kontoleon/Macrory/Swanson, Individual Preference-based Values and Environmental Decision Making: Should Valuation Have Its Day in Court? Research in Law and Economics, Vol 20, 2020, 179.

Lienbacher, Abwägungsentscheidungen im öffentlichen Recht, in *Khakzadeh-Leiler/ Schmid/Weber* (eds), Interessenabwägung und Abwägungsentscheidungen, Forschungen aus Staat und Recht, Band 175 (2014) 85.

Madner/Schulev-Steindl, Dritte Piste – Klimaschutz als Willkür? Anmerkungen zu VfGH 29 June 2017, E 875/2017, E 886/2017, ZÖR 2017, 589.

Merli, Ein seltsamer Fall von Willkür: Die VfGH-Entscheidung zur dritten Piste des Flughafens Wien, wbl 2017, 682.

Niederhuber, Dritte-Piste-Entscheidung zeigt: Es gilt das Gesetz, DerStandard 2017/36/01.

Perman et al, Natural Resource and Environmental Economics (2011).

Schmelz, Der VfGH zur dritten Piste – Klimaschutz im Widerspruch zu Rechtsstaat und Demokratie? ZGV 2017, 288.

Schulev-Steindl/Romirer, Interessenabwägung im Vorarlberger Naturschutz- recht – Funktionen, Dimensionen und Evaluierung (2019), www.naturschutzrat.at/studien/.

Schulev-Steindl/Romirer, Interessenabwägung im Naturschutzrecht – Ein Problemaufriss am Beispiel Vorarlbergs, RdU 2020, 187.

Steininger, Die gesamtwirtschaftlichen Folgekosten des klimapolitischen Nicht-Handelns am Beispiel Österreich, in *Kirchengast/Schulev-Steindl/Schnedl* (eds), Klimaschutzrecht zwischen Wunsch und Wirklichkeit (2018) 33.

Sturm/Vogt, Umweltökonomik. Eine anwendungsorientierte Einführung (2011).

Uerpmann, Das öffentliche Interesse (1999).

Wagner, Was bislang geschah: Staatszieldebatte/VfGH hebt Urteil Dritte Piste auf, RdU 2017, 149.

CASES

BVwG 2 February 2017, W109 2000179-1.

VfGH 29 June 2017, E 875/2017, E 886/2017.

VwGH 6 March 2019, Ro 2017/03/0031.

VwGH 9 June 2020, Ra 2019/10/0075.

VwGH 16 December 2019, Ra 2018/03/0066.

VwGH 9 November 2016, Ro 2014/10/0044.

VwGH 18 February 2015, 2013/10/0074.

VwGH 24 January 2013, 2011/07/0252.

VwGH 2 January 2010, 2008/07/0033.

VwGH 02 October 2007, 2004/10/0174.

Resettlements as Spatial Adaptation Measures to Tackle Climate Change Impacts?

Markus Scharler[*]

1   Natural Science Foundations

Austria has experienced more negative impacts of climate change in recent years, leading to recurring natural disasters with increasing frequency. Given the current state of knowledge, there will most likely be significantly more temperature extremes in Austria in the 21st century. In particular, torrential rain and devastating storms bear significant destructive potential.[1] Austria has already witnessed numerous devastating floods in recent years. As a result of the devastating floods in 2002 and 2013 in the Eferding Basin (Lower Austria), communities have faced and still face environmentally induced resettlements. However, these resettlements were executed on the basis of voluntary agreements with the Austrian state, which are governed by private law.[2] Moreover, it is assumed that the thawing permafrost (provoked mainly by climate change) will lead to more frequent and more severe landslides and rockfalls, inevitably leading to more resettlement cases.[3]

It is generally noted that climate change research may be characterised by various uncertainties, in contrast to other natural science disciplines.[4] However, there is a strong consensus in the international scientific community about the anthropogenic cause of climate change.[5] In view of the complexity of climate change (e.g. the existence of countless emitters of carbon dioxide (CO_2), the traceability of the CO_2 emissions to individual disasters), it is often difficult to make accurate statements in the field of climate change

---

[*] This article offers a brief look at the author's dissertation (Climate Change, Space, and Adaptation from the Perspective of Law) and is mostly adapted from the blog post previously published in 2020: *Scharler*, Absiedlung als raumbezogene Anpassungsmaßnahme an den Klimawandel?, JuWissBlog Nr. 90/2020 v. 18 June 2020, www.juwiss.de/90-2020/ (last accessed 20 February 2021).

[1] *APCC*, Österreichischer Sachstandsbericht Klimawandel (2014) 302.

[2] *Cf.* instead of many reports in the extensive media coverage www.derstandard.at/story/2000011527317/ eferdinger-becken-hochwasseropfer-stimmen-absiedlung-zu (last accessed 20 February 2021).

[3] *Schindelegger*, Absiedlung als Planungsinstrument. Planerische Aspekte zu Siedlungsrückzug als Naturgefahrenprävention (2019) Dissertation Wien, 22 und 51.

[4] *See* several dissertations in DK Climate Change alone, https://dk-climate-change.uni-graz.at/de/forschung/ dissertationsprojekte/ (last accessed 20 February 2021).

[5] *Kirchengast*, Wissenstand der Klimaforschung und Herausforderung Klimaschutz: Können wir den Klimawandel noch bremsen?, in Kirchengast/Schulev-Steindl/Schnedl (eds), Klimaschutzrecht zwischen Wunsch und Wirklichkeit (2018) 11 (14).

research. For this reason, the extent to which resettlement measures can be reconciled with the uncertainties mentioned must also be taken into account when analysing state protection measures.

2   State Obligation to Protect?

Against this background, the question arises as to whether and to what extent the state is required to undertake spatial adaption measures, such as resettlement programmes, in order to tackle the adverse impacts of climate change. In this context, resettlement is considered as the state's intentional and permanent abandonment of housing or residence of individuals (or groups) in a certain area to mitigate climate change-induced hazards. One cannot deduce a general state obligation to resettle people owing to climate change solely on the basis of the fact that there have been several international and national cases of resettlement. From a domestic Austrian legal point of view, there is no obligation to carry out resettlement purely on the basis of macroeconomic costs or cost considerations related to the individual case because there is, in principle, no legal basis for it.[6] Principles of environmental law, such as the precautionary principle or the polluter-pays principle, also lack the capacity to establish a state obligation to protect. Although all of these arguments are politically and factually inherent to the resettlement debate, they provide no ground for establishing the state's obligation to take such intrusive measures.

As a matter of fact, the increasing number of natural disasters occurring in the Alpine region pose a danger to human life,[7] in response to which the state is obliged to take some sort of protective measures. The questions arise as to the extent to which and the way in which the state has to counter the adverse climate-induced impacts. In this context, it is necessary to examine whether the obligations of the state within the human rights framework and, in particular, the state's obligation to protect, may validly answer these questions. This is discussed in what follows.

3   The Obligation to Protect Under the Human Rights Framework

In recent times, the climate lawsuits against states have relied on the state responsibility with regard to climate change established by human rights frameworks.[8] The fact that the

---

6   Admittedly, especially in passive flood protection, resettlement will often be more favourable than particularly complex technical protective measures designed for limited durations, cf. *Schindelegger*, Absiedlung 7.

7   *Rottenwallner*, Die Schutzpflichtendogmatik und das neue Sicherheitsdenken, ZÖR 2017, 469 (483 f) even sees 'climate-evoked' catastrophes as one of the central threats of our time.

8   *See Gabler/Senders*, Kann man Klimaschutz einklagen?, JuWissBlog Nr. 118/2019 v. 13.12.2019, www.juwiss.de/118-2019/ (last accessed 20 February 2021); *Schnedl*, Die Rolle der Gerichte im Klimaschutz,

state is obliged to protect its citizens under certain circumstances is no longer in doubt. However, there is no broad consensus on the extent and scope of this state responsibility, in particular, the ways in which the state has to protect certain communities that are vulnerable to climate-induced natural disasters.

The human rights framework established under the European Convention on Human Rights (ECHR), which has the status of constitutional law in Austria, is the strongest legal basis on which to establish a state obligation to protect. The right to life (Art. 2 ECHR), the freedom of property (Art. 1 1. CPR) as well as the right to respect for private and family life and, in particular, the right to respect for the home (Art. 8 ECHR) are inherent to resettlement issues. The European Court of Human Rights (ECtHR) is considered to play a pivotal role in setting obligatory standards of protection for states.[9]

In the case of *Budayeva and others v. Russia*,[10] the ECtHR found that the state has an obligation to protect against natural hazards (in that case a mudslide), without requiring attribution to third parties. The ECtHR recognised that Russia violated its obligation to protect under Article 2 ECHR. In casu, Russia's authorities set up neither an early warning system nor a sufficient legal and administrative framework. As to the latter, the regional spatial authorities and the legislative authorities failed to take measures to mitigate the foreseeable risk to the applicants' lives.

In conjunction with other judgments of the ECtHR (*Öneryildiz v. Turkey*[11] and *Kolyadenko and others v. Russia*[12]), one can validly conclude that the state has a broad margin of discretion in choosing the protective measures to tackle climate-induced natural disasters. However, this broad margin of discretion is limited by the requirement of practical utility, as pointed out by the ECtHR in numerous judgments.[13] Therefore, the protective measures taken by the state must have the capacity to effectively contribute to the protection of human life, the home and property. The state may certainly take a wide variety of effective measures subject to the condition that they fulfil its obligation to protect under the ECHR.

4   LIMITS TO THE OBLIGATION TO PROTECT?

But is the most effective protection to be guaranteed at any price? According to the legal paradigm *ultra posse nemo obligatur*, the state is not required to take impossible or

---

in Kirchengast/Schulev-Steindl/Schnedl (Hrsg), Klimaschutzrecht zwischen Wunsch und Wirklichkeit 128; *Schulev-Steindl*, Klimaklagen: Ein Trend erreicht Österreich, ecolex 2021/7, 17.

9   *See Khakzadeh-Leiler*, Die Grundrechte in der Judikatur des Obersten Gerichtshofs (2011) 28.

10   ECHR 20 March 2008, 15339/02 (*Budayeva et al v. Russia*).

11   ECHR 30 November 2004, 48939/99 (*Öneryildiz v. Turkey*).

12   ECHR 28.02.2012, 17423/05 (*Kolyadenko et al v. Russia*).

13   *See Kneihs*, Grundrechte und Sterbehilfe (1998) 74.

disproportionate measures to comply with its obligations. Additionally, according to the principle of subsidiarity, the communities affected by natural disasters are also required to take non-excessive measures to provide for themselves.[14] Admittedly, this requirement is vague and must therefore always be measured against each individual case. The state should conduct a proportionality test, taking due account of the present circumstances. The complexity of the case, the severity of the human rights infringement as well as the number of legal interests at stake shall be considered. Likewise, conflicting human rights positions should also be taken into consideration. Since the best possible protection is to be guaranteed, the state should take the measure of resettlement as an *ultima ratio*.[15]

5   CONCLUSION

As far as I am concerned, the state shall prefer a set of low-impact measures over one particularly severe measure, such as resettlement programmes, when it comes to combating climate change. The *ultima ratio* character of resettlement programmes rests on two grounds: on the one hand, it is the last resort in an overall catalogue of measures. On the other hand, within a potential resettlement regime, the state should adopt less intrusive (meaning private-sector) resettlement measures, such as subsidies or contracts, rather than more intrusive instruments, such as property restrictions or expropriations.

BIBLIOGRAPHY

APCC, Österreichischer Sachstandsbericht Klimawandel (2014).

Berka, Verfassungsrecht[7] (2018).

Doctoral Programme Climate Change, University of Graz, PhD Projects, https://dk-climate-change.uni-graz.at/de/forschung/dissertationsprojekte/ (last accessed 20 February 2021).

Gabler/Senders, Kann man Klimaschutz einklagen? JuWissBlog Nr. 118/2019 v. 13.12.2019, www.juwiss.de/118-2019/ (last accessed 20 February 2021).

Khakzadeh-Leiler, Die Grundrechte in der Judikatur des Obersten Gerichtshofs (2011).

---

14   *Rottenwallner*, ZÖR 2017, 469 (481).
15   *See Berka*, Verfassungsrecht[7] (2018) Rz 1224; *Szczekalla*, Die sogenannten grundrechtlichen Schutzpflichten im deutschen und europäischen Recht (2002) 176.

Kirchengast, Wissenstand der Klimaforschung und Herausforderung Klimaschutz: Können wir den Klimawandel noch bremsen?, in *Kirchengast/Schulev-Steindl/Schnedl* (eds), Klimaschutzrecht zwischen Wunsch und Wirklichkeit (2018) 11.

Kneihs, Grundrechte und Sterbehilfe (1998).

Mathofer, Isle de Jean Charles: Untergang einer Insel, www.dw.com/de/isle-de-jean-charles-untergang-einer-insel/a-19239211 (11 May 2016).

Rohrhofer, Eferdinger Becken: Hochwasseropfer stimmen Absiedelung zu, www.derstandard.at/story/2000011527317/eferdinger-becken-hochwasseropfer-stimmen-absiedlung-zu (10 February 2015).

Rottenwallner, Die Schutzpflichtendogmatik und das neue Sicherheitsdenken, ZÖR 2017, 469.

Scharler, Absiedlung als raumbezogene Anpassungsmaßnahme an den Klimawandel? JuWissBlog Nr. 90/2020 v. 18 June 2020, www.juwiss.de/90-2020/ (last accessed 20 February 2021).

Schindelegger, Absiedlung als Planungsinstrument. Planerische Aspekte zu Siedlungsrückzug als Naturgefahrenprävention (2019) Dissertation Vienna.

Schnedl, Die Rolle der Gerichte im Klimaschutz, in *Kirchengast/Schulev-Steindl/Schnedl* (eds), Klimaschutzrecht zwischen Wunsch und Wirklichkeit (2018) 128.

Schulev-Steindl, Klimaklagen: Ein Trend erreicht Österreich, ecolex 2021/7, 17.

Schwarz, Alaska: Ein Dorf flieht vor dem Klimawandel, www.klimaretter.info/umwelt/hintergrund/21767-alaska-ein-dorf-flieht-vor-dem-klimawandel (20 August 2016).

Szczekalla, Die sogenannten grundrechtlichen Schutzpflichten im deutschen und europäischen Recht (2002).

Cases

Bundesgericht (Schweiz) 14 July 2015, 1C_567/2014.

ECHR 20 March 2008, 15339/02 (*Budayeva et al v. Russia*).

ECHR 30 November 2004, 48939/99 (*Öneryildiz v. Turkey*).

ECHR 28 February 2012, 17423/05 (*Kolyadenko et al v. Russia*).

The European Green Deal – What Is in a Name?

Isabel Staudinger[*]

1 Introduction

Since early 2020, the economy has been affected by the measures taken to combat the COVID-19 pandemic. Yet the economic shutdown also brought a reduction in greenhouse gas emissions and thus an unexpected recovery for the environment.[1] Besides, government rescue measures at the European Union (EU) level increasingly paid attention to compliance with climate protection measures. On the national level, for example, Air France was requested in 2020 to abolish domestic flights[2] and, in 2021, the German Green party announced a similar strategy.[3] The demand for fleet renewal by Lufthansa[4] paired with competition law requirements of the European Commission (Commission)[5] was probably a little less targeted.

---

[*] A first version of this contribution has been published in June 2020 (Isabel Staudinger, Der europäische Grüne Deal: Übergang zu Klimaneutralität und nachhaltiger Entwicklung unter Einhaltung der Rechtsstaatlichkeit (JuWissBlog Nr. 88/2020 v. 18.06.2020), https://www.juwiss.de/88-2020/). The author would like to thank Mag. Emil Nigmatullin, Lydia Omuku-Jung, LL.M., and Mag.[a] Julia Wallner for the organisation of this volume, their valuable comments, and the language review. The author expresses gratitude to Léo Gotarda, LL.B LL.M. MA, Univ.-Prof. Dr. András Jakab, LL.M., PhD, Prof. PD. Dr. Lando Kirchmair, Mag. Sebastian Krempelmeier, BA, and Univ.-Prof. MMMag. Dr. Rainer Palmstorfer, LL.M. (Sacramento) for their critique, comments, and suggestions.

[1] *Le Quéré/Jackson/Jones et al*, Temporary reduction in daily global CO2 emissions during the COVID-19 forced confinement, Nature Climate Change 2020, 647. Available at www.nature.com/articles/s41558-020-0797-x (19 May 2020). On Austria, e.g., *WIFO*, Treibhausgasemissionen werden in Österreich 2020 zumindest um 7.1% abnehmen, www.wifo.ac.at/news/treibhausgasemissionen_werden_in_oesterreich_2020_zumindest_um_71_abnehmen (10 May 2020).

[2] *Der Spiegel*, Air France soll Inlandsflüge zugunsten von Schnellzügen streichen. Available at www.spiegel.de/auto/air-france-soll-inlandsfluege-zugunsten-von-schnellzuegen-streichen-a-a1dabbeb-9e61-43ab-b707-09378a5a3616 (5 May 2020).

[3] *Die Zeit*, Annalena Baerbock will Kurzstreckenflüge auf Dauer abschaffen. Available at www.zeit.de/politik/deutschland/2021-05/gruene-annalena-baerbock-kurzstreckenfluege-solar-kimaschutz (16 May 2021).

[4] *Süddeutsche Zeitung*, Bund stellt Umweltauflagen für Lufthansa-Rettungspaket. Available at www.sueddeutsche.de/wirtschaft/luftverkehr-frankfurt-am-main-bund-stellt-umweltauflagen-fuer-lufthansa-rettungspaket-dpa.urn-newsml-dpa-com-20090101-200525-99-182542 (25 May 2020).

[5] *Frankfurter Allgemeine Zeitung*, Lufthansa will Auflagen der EU-Kommission annehmen. Available at www.faz.net/aktuell/wirtschaft/unternehmen/regierung-und-eu-kommission-einigen-sich-bei-lufthansa-rettung-16793046.html (30 May 2020).

The implementation of the European Green Deal,[6] a new growth strategy that was adopted at the end of 2019, takes place in light of the new economic and environmental challenges that have arisen. This is also shown in the novel recital (1a), which has been proposed with the adjustment of the multiannual financial framework (MFF) 2021-2027. The recital states that "[t]he economic impact of the COVID-19 crisis requires the Union to provide a long-term financial framework paving the way to a fair and inclusive transition to a green and digital future, supporting the Union's longer-term strategic autonomy and making it resilient to shocks in the future."[7]

During the year 2020, the Commission adopted a series of communications and proposals to breathe life into the Green Deal (2). Thus, the following section briefly discusses the EU's road to climate neutrality and the implementation of the Paris Agreement and the Sustainable Development Goals (SDGs)[8] (2.1). Next, the financial instrument elements of the Green Deal are analysed with regard to their 'greenness', i.e. the extent to which they are supposed to contribute to the protection of the environment and sustainable development (2.2). Based on that analysis, several peculiarities of these financial instruments that allow for further research are addressed (3). To this end, the objectives and spending criteria relating to the protection of the environment and sustainable development (3.1), their legal bases and their source of funds in form of the Recovery and Resilience Facility[9] (3.2), and the reference to the newly adopted regime on conditionality in Regulation (EU, Euratom) 2020/2092[10] (3.3) are screened.

2   The European Green Deal

The title 'European Green Deal' is reminiscent of the 1933 'New Deal', initiated under the administration of the former president of the United States, Franklin D. Roosevelt. According to the European Commission, the European Green Deal "is a new growth strategy that aims to transform the EU into a fair and prosperous society, with a modern, resource-efficient and competitive economy where there are no net emissions of greenhouse gases in 2050 and where economic growth is decoupled from resource use".[11] The

---

6   Communication from the Commission, The European Green Deal, COM (2019) 640 final of 11 December 2019.
7   Amended proposal for a Council Regulation laying down the multiannual financial framework for the years 2021 to 2027, COM (2020) 442 final of 28 May 2020.
8   *United Nations Department of Economic and Social Affairs*, Sustainable Development Goals. Available at https://sdgs.un.org (6 June 2020).
9   Regulation (EU) 2020/2094 of the Council of 14 December 2020, establishing a European Union Recovery Instrument to support the recovery in the aftermath of the COVID-19 crisis, OJ 2020 L 433I/23.
10   Regulation (EU, Euratom) 2020/2092 of the European Parliament and of the Council of 16 December 2020 on a general regime of conditionality for the protection of the Union budget, OJ 2020 L 433I/1.
11   COM (2019) 640 final, p. 1.

Commission described the European Green Deal in the respective communication as "an integral part of the Commission's strategy to implement the United Nation's 2030 Agenda and the sustainable development goals".[12] As early as in 2018, the EU Commission had set the goal of achieving a climate-neutral economy by 2050.[13] It initiated Regulation (EU) 2018/1999 on the Governance of the Energy Union and Climate Action.[14] Thus, the question arises as to whether or not the European Green is as 'green' as the title suggests. 'Green' is to be understood as follows: in what way is the disbursement of funds made conditional on fulfilling certain criteria that demand any contribution to environmental protection and/or sustainable development? To answer this question, some light must be shed on the development of the European Green Deal.

2.1   The Road to Climate Neutrality

The 17 goals for sustainable development, better known as SDGs,[15] were mentioned only in half-sentences in the EU's policies at the beginning. Other areas of EU law, such as the EU's external action, similarly did not include a comprehensive implementation of the SDGs.[16] In 2019, however, the European Semester intended to integrate the SDGs in the framework of macroeconomic coordination, "to put sustainability and the well-being of citizens at the centre of economic policy, and the sustainable development goals at the heart of the EU's policymaking and action".[17] SDG No. 13 (Climate Action) aims, inter alia, to integrate climate protection measures into national policies, strategies and planning and to curb climate change. The requirement of sustainable development – together with environmental protection – forms one of the EU's objectives (Article 3(3) TFEU)[18] and part of the legally binding cross-sectional clause of Article 11 TFEU on compliance with

---

12   COM (2019) 640 final, recital (1a).
13   Communication from the Commission to the European Parliament, the European Council, the Council, the European Economic and Social Committee, the Committee of the Regions and the European Investment Bank, A Clean Planet for all. A European strategic long-term vision for a prosperous, modern, competitive and climate-neutral economy, COM (2018) 773 final, 28 November 2018.
14   Regulation (EU) 2018/1999 of the European Parliament and of the Council of 11 December 2018 on the Governance of the Energy Union and Climate Action, amending Regulations (EC) 663/2009 and (EC) 715/2009 of the European Parliament and of the Council, Directives 94/22/EC, 98/70/EC, 2009/31/EC, 2009/73/EC, 2010/31/EU, 2012/27/EU and 2013/30/EU of the European Parliament and of the Council, Council Directives 2009/119/EC and (EU) 2015/652 and repealing Regulation (EU) 525/2013 of the European Parliament and of the Council, OJ 2018 L 328/1.
15   Formulated in United Nations General Assembly, Transforming our world: the 2030 Agenda for Sustainable Development (adopted on 25 September 2015) A/RES/71/1.
16   On the (non-)implementation of the SDGs by the EU in its relationship with third countries to date, *see, e.g., Huck*, Die EU und die Globale Agenda 2030 der Vereinten Nationen: Reflexion, Strategie und rechtliche Umsetzung, EuZW 2019, 581.
17   COM(2019) 640 final, p. 3.
18   Treaty on the Functioning of the European Union.

environmental protection.[19] Thus, the connection between sustainable economic development and environmental protection already stems from EU primary law. Until 2020, the main instrument was the programme for environmental and climate policy (LIFE), under which EUR 5.45 billion is allocated towards undertaking the "shift towards a resource-efficient, low-carbon and climate-resilient economy, to the protection and improvement of the quality of the environment and to halting and reversing biodiversity loss" and the "development, implementation and enforcement of Union environmental and climate policy and legislation".[20]

At this point, the international climate frameworks such as the United Nations Framework Convention on Climate Change (1992),[21] the Kyoto Protocol (1997)[22] and the Paris Agreement (2015)[23] must also be borne in mind. In its communication on a modern budget, the initial proposal for the new 2021 to 2027 MFF,[24] the EU Commission considered the Paris Agreement and the SDGs and proposed "to set a more ambitious goal for climate mainstreaming across all EU programmes, with a target of 25% of EU expenditure contributing to climate objectives".[25]

In late 2020, the Commission announced several initial climate actions under the European Green Deal:[26] the European Climate Law shall be based on Articles 191 to 193 TFEU and targets the achievement of climate neutrality.[27] The European Climate Pact

---

19 *Huck*, EuZW 2019, 582f. On the binding legal nature of Art. 11 TFEU, *see e.g.*, *Krämer*, Artikel 11 [Umweltschutz; Querschnittsklausel], in *Groeben/Schwarze/Hatje* (eds), Europäisches Unionsrecht[7] 2015 para 25.

20 Regulation (EU) 2013/1293 of the European Parliament and of the Council of 11 December 2013 on the establishment of a Programme for the Environment and Climate Action (LIFE) and repealing Regulation (EC) 614/2007, OJ 2013 L 347/185, Art. 3(1)(a) and (b). *See also* (c) and (d).

21 United Nations Framework Convention on Climate Change (adopted 9 May 1992, entered into force on 21 March 1994) 1771 UNTS 107.

22 Kyoto Protocol to the United Nations Framework Convention on Climate Change (adopted 11 December 1997, entered into force on 16 February 2005) 2303 UNTS 148.

23 Conference of the Parties, Adoption of the Paris Agreement (adopted on 12 December 2015) UN Doc FCCC/CP/2015/L.9/Rev/1.

24 Proposal for a Council Regulation laying down the multiannual financial framework for the years 2021 to 2027, COM (2018) 322 final of 2 May 2018.

25 Communication from the Commission to the European Parliament, the European Council, the Council, the European Economic and Social Committee and the Committee of the Regions, A Modern Budget for a Union that Protects, Empowers and Defends the Multiannual Financial Framework for 2021-2027, COM (2018) 321 final of 2 May 2018, p. 15.

26 *European Commission*, EU climate action and the European Green Deal. Available at https://ec.europa.eu/clima/policies/eu-climate-action_en (6 June 2021).

27 Proposal for a Regulation of the European Parliament and of the Council establishing the framework for achieving climate neutrality and amending Regulation (EU) 2018/1999 (European Climate Law), COM (2020) 80 final of 4 March 2020. Adopted as Regulation (EU) 2021/1119 of the European Parliament and of the Council of 30 June 2021 establishing the framework for achieving climate neutrality and amending Regulations (EC) No 401/2009 and (EU) 2018/1999 ('European Climate Law') [2021] OJ L243/1.

provides for the connection of EU citizens to develop climate solutions.[28] The 2030 Climate Target Plan addresses the reduction of greenhouse gas emissions.[29] In addition, the year 2021 became the European Year of the Rail,[30] and the Commission put in place a circular economy action plan.[31] In several cases, explicit references were made to the European Green Deal and to the associated goal of achieving climate neutrality by 2050.[32] In 2021, the Commission adopted a new EU strategy on adaptation to climate change, explaining the role and necessity of these climate actions.[33] Thereby, the European Green Deal, in principle, marks the beginning of a new development, where the EU's objective of sustainable development and environmental protection is to be articulated in (directly applicable) secondary EU legislation.

2.2 Elements of a Just Green Transition

In addition to the programmatic communication on the European Green Deal, a corresponding road map was formulated at the end of 2019,[34] which was supplemented by an investment plan in January 2020.[35] Later, the European Green Deal was equipped with several legislative proposals in the area of financial assistance in May 2020. The proposals include the following: first, the establishment of a Recovery and Resilience Facility[36] to support economic, territorial and social cohesion by mitigating the effects of

---

28 Communication from the Commission to the European Parliament, the Council, the European Economic and Social Committee and the Committee of the Regions, European Climate Pact, COM (2020) 788 final of 9 December 2020.

29 Communication from the Commission to the European Parliament, the Council, the European Council, the European Economic and Social Committee and the Committee of the Regions, Stepping up Europe's 2030 climate ambition. Investing in a climate-neutral future for the benefit of our people, COM (2020) 562 final of 17 September 2020.

30 Decision (EU) 2020/2228 of the European Parliament and of the Council of 23 December 2020 on a European Year of Rail (2021), OJ 2020 L 437/108.

31 Communication from the Commission to the European Parliament, the Council, the European Economic and Social Committee and the Committee of the Regions, A new Circular Economy Action Plan For a cleaner and more competitive Europe, COM (2020) 98 final of 11 March 2020.

32 Regulation (EU) 1293/2013, recital (18); Decision (EU) 2020/2228, recitals (1) to (5); COM (2020) 98 final, p. 2 f; Regulation (EU) 2018/1999, recital (10) and Art. 15(2)(a).

33 Communication from the Commission to the European Parliament, the Council, the European Economic and Social Committee and the Committee of the Regions, Forging a climate-resilient Europe – the new EU Strategy on Adaptation to Climate Change, COM (2021) 82 final of 24 February 2021.

34 COM (2019) 640 final, ANNEX.

35 Communication from the Commission to the European Parliament, the Council, the European Economic and Social Committee and the Committee of the Regions, Sustainable Europe Investment Plan European Green Deal Investment Plan, COM (2020) 21 final of 14 January 2020.

36 Regulation (EU) 2021/241 of the European Parliament and of the Council of 12 February 2021, establishing the Recovery and Resilience Facility, OJ 2021 L 57/17.

the green transition.[37] Second, there was an increase in the resources for the EU funds (REACT-EU),[38] where Article 92b was inserted in Regulation (EU) 1303/2013.[39] Third, a mechanism was put in place for a just transition, which itself consists of three components:[40] (i) a Just Transition Fund, is intended to address socio-economic challenges to cushion the transition to a climate-neutral economy.[41] (ii) A Just Transition scheme (a special Regulation within the framework of InvestEU) should ensure the sustainability of the Union's economy and its environmental and climate dimensions. The scheme should, inter alia, contribute to the achievement of the SDGs and the goals of the Paris Agreement on Climate Change and to the creation of high-quality jobs.[42] (iii) A public sector loan facility, together with the European Investment Bank (EIB), which has referred to itself since November 2019 as the 'EU Climate Bank',[43] has been adopted for the support of public authorities in the transition.[44]

3   THREE PECULIARITIES OF THE EUROPEAN GREEN DEAL

An examination of the financial instruments of the European Green Deal shows at least three peculiarities that are worth discussing: (1) Competences, objectives and spending criteria relating to the protection of the environment and sustainable development limit the allocation of funds. (2) Financing of the European Green Deal is largely based on the Recovery Instrument. (3) The instruments of the European Green Deal contain references

---

37 Regulation (EU) 2021/241, Arts. 3 and 4.

38 Regulation (EU) 2020/2221 of the European Parliament and of the Council of 23 December 2020 amending Regulation (EU) 1303/2013 as regards additional resources and implementing arrangements to provide assistance for fostering crisis repair in the context of the COVID-19 pandemic and its social consequences and for preparing a green, digital and resilient recovery of the economy (REACT-EU), OJ 2020 L 437/30.

39 Regulation (EU) 2013/1303 of the European Parliament and of the Council of 17 December 2013, laying down common provisions on the European Regional Development Fund, the European Social Fund, the Cohesion Fund, the European Agricultural Fund for Rural Development and the European Maritime and Fisheries Fund and laying down general provisions on the European Regional Development Fund, the European Social Fund, the Cohesion Fund and the European Maritime and Fisheries Fund and repealing Council Regulation (EC) 1083/2006, OJ 2013 L 347/320.

40 *European Commission*, The Just Transition Mechanism: making sure no one is left behind. Available at https://ec.europa.eu/info/strategy/priorities-2019-2024/european-green-deal/actions-being-taken-eu/just-transition-mechanism_en (6 June 2021).

41 Regulation (EU) 2021/1056 of the European Parliament and of the Council of 24 June 2021 establishing the Just Transition Fund [2021] OJ L 231/1.

42 Regulation (EU) 2021/523 of the European Parliament and of the Council of 24 March 2021, establishing the InvestEU Programme and amending Regulation (EU) 2015/1017, OJ 2021 L 107/30, Art. 3 (1) lit b.

43 *European Investment Bank*, EU Bank launches ambitious new climate strategy and Energy Lending Policy. Available at www.eib.org/en/press/all/2019-313-eu-bank-launches-ambitious-new-climate-strategy-and-energy-lending-policy (14 November 2019).

44 Regulation (EU) 2021/1229 of the European Parliament and of the Council of 14 July 2021 on the public sector loan facility under the Just Transition Mechanism [2021] OJ L 274/, Art. 1.

to the general regime of conditionality for the protection of the Union budget in Regulation (EU, Euratom) 2020/2092. While the latter finding is a mere decoration, the former two peculiarities allow for an assessment of the 'green' element in the European Green Deal.

3.1 Objectives and Spending Criteria Relating to the Protection of the Environment and Sustainable Development

An examination of the objectives and spending criteria of the financial instruments reveals interesting insights into the question of how 'green' the European Green Deal really is. An initial assessment is to determine the share of resources to be spent on climate objectives. In the initial proposals, e.g. on the Just Transition Fund, an "overall target of 25% of the Union budget expenditure contributing to climate objectives"[45] was included. As mentioned in the recitals of the Recovery and Resilience Facility[46] and the InvestEU,[47] that overall share has been increased to 30%. As regards REACT-EU, "the Funds will contribute to mainstream climate actions and to the achievement of an overall target of 30% of the Union budget expenditure supporting climate objectives. REACT-EU is expected to contribute 25% of the overall financial envelope to climate objectives".[48] The Regulation on the public sector loan facility does not contain a similar reference.

Beyond that, the financial instruments can be classified into three groups. The first contains cohesion measures in response to the COVID-19 pandemic. These measures contain the secondary objective of preparing a green, digital and resilient recovery of the economy. The Recovery and Resilience Facility's general objective is to promote the Union's economic, social and territorial cohesion in the light of the COVID-19 pandemic, "by supporting the green transition, by contributing to the achievement of the Union's 2030 climate targets set out in point (11) of Article 2 of Regulation (EU) 2018/1999 and by complying with the objective of EU climate neutrality by 2050 [...]."[49] In addition, Article 5 of Regulation (EU) 2021/241 determines that "the Facility shall only support measures respecting the principle of 'do no significant harm'".[50] According to recital (23) of Regulation (EU) 2021/241, the 'do no significant harm' principle is defined in Article 17 of Regulation (EU) 2020/852,[51] which refers to Article 2(17) of Regulation (EU) 2019/2088,

---

45 For example, COM (2020) 22 final, recital (6).
46 Regulation (EU) 2021/241, recital (23).
47 Regulation (EU) 2021/523, recital (10).
48 Regulation (EU) 2020/2221, recital (6).
49 Regulation (EU) 2021/241, Art. 4(2).
50 Regulation (EU) 2021/241, Art. 5(2).
51 Regulation (EU) 2020/852 of the European Parliament and of the Council of 18 June 2020 on the establishment of a framework to facilitate sustainable investment, and amending Regulation (EU) 2019/2088, OJ 2020 L 198/13.

stipulating that sustainable investments must not do significant harm to any of (e.g.) environmental objectives,[52] without defining the term 'significant harm'. By the same token, Article 92b (8) of Regulation (EU) 1303/2013 defines the following: "The REACT-EU resources not allocated to technical assistance shall be used under the thematic objective referred to in the first subparagraph of paragraph 9 to support operations that foster crisis repair in the context of the COVID-19 pandemic and its social consequences and prepare a green, digital and resilient recovery of the economy.[53] Recital (18) mentions that "REACT-EU resources should be used in accordance with the sustainable development and 'Do no harm' principles".[54]

The second group contains only the InvestEU Programme, of which sustainability and the environment are only at the centre of a fraction of funds. Article 3 of InvestEU defines the following: "The general objective of the InvestEU Programme is to support the policy objectives of the Union by means of financing and investment operations that contribute to: [...] (b) growth and employment in the Union economy, the sustainability of the Union economy and its environmental and climate dimension contributing to the achievement of the SDGs and the objectives of the Paris Agreement and to the creation of high-quality jobs."[55] Moreover, Annex II enlists areas eligible for financial and investment operations, which "may include strategic investment to support final recipients whose activities are of strategic importance to the Union, in particular in view of the green and digital transitions, of enhanced resilience and of strengthening strategic value chains".[56] Among these areas, four contain a specific link to the protection of the environment:

1. "clean energy transition and the commitments taken under the 2030 Agenda for Sustainable Development and the Paris Agreement [...]

---

52 Regulation (EU) 2019/2088 of the European Parliament and of the Council of 27 November 2019 on sustainability - related disclosures in the financial services sector, OJ 2019 L317/1, Art. 2(17): "'sustainable investment' means an investment in an economic activity that contributes to an environmental objective, as measured, for example, by key resource efficiency indicators on the use of energy, renewable energy, raw materials, water and land, on the production of waste, and greenhouse gas emissions, or on its impact on biodiversity and the circular economy, or an investment in an economic activity that contributes to a social objective, in particular an investment that contributes to tackling inequality or that fosters social cohesion, social integration and labour relations, or an investment in human capital or economically or socially disadvantaged communities, provided that such investments do not significantly harm any of those objectives and that the investee companies follow good governance practices, in particular with respect to sound management structures, employee relations, remuneration of staff and tax compliance."

53 Regulation (EU) 2020/2221, Art. 1. A similar expression can be found in Art. 92a of Regulation 1303/2013: "These additional resources for 2021 and 2022, stemming from the European Union Recovery Instrument, shall provide assistance for fostering crisis repair in the context of the COVID-19 pandemic and its social consequences and for preparing a green, digital and resilient recovery of the economy ('REACT-EU resources')."

54 Regulation (EU) 2020/2221, recital (18).

55 Regulation (EU) 2021/523, Art. 3.

56 Regulation (EU) 2021/523, Annex II.

2. the development of sustainable and safe transport infrastructures and mobility solutions, equipment and innovative technologies in accordance with Union transport priorities and the commitments taken under the Paris Agreement [...]
3. environment and resources [...]
4. sustainable agriculture, forestry, fishery, aquaculture and other elements of the wider sustainable bioeconomy [...]"

The third group includes measures to mitigate the challenges of transitioning towards a climate-neutral economy: A Just Transition Fund "shall contribute to the single specific objective of enabling regions and people to address the social, employment, economic and environmental impacts of the transition towards the Union's 2030 targets for energy and climate and a climate-neutral economy of the Union by 2050, based on the Paris Agreement.".[57] In the same vein, the envisaged public sector loan facility has a similar general objective, namely to "address serious social, economic and environmental challenges deriving from the transition towards the Union's 2030 climate and energy targets and the objective of climate neutrality".[58] Correspondingly, Article 8 of Regulation (EU) 2021/1229 defines four criteria for the eligibility of the projects, the first of which states that "the projects achieve a measurable impact, and include output indicators where appropriate, in addressing serious social, economic and environmental challenges deriving from the transition towards the Union's 2030 climate and energy targets and the objective of climate neutrality in the Union by 2050 at the latest and benefit territories identified in a territorial just transition plan, even if the projects are not located in those territories".[59]

In sum, the protection of the environment and sustainable environment seem to be a by-product rather than the main objective of the European Green Deal's financial instruments. With a minimum requirement of 25 to 30% of funds dedicated to climate objectives, that share is rather low, which is also reflected in the design of spending criteria. The remaining funds of the Recovery and Resilience Facility and of REACT-EU shall comply with the 'do no harm' principle. However, that principle prohibits only 'significant' harm – a term yet to be defined.

---

57 Regulation (EU) 2021/1056, Art. 2. Also reflected in Art. 1(1): "This Regulation establishes the Just Transition Fund (JTF) to provide support to the people, economies and environment of territories which face serious socio-economic challenges deriving from the transition process towards the Union's 2030 targets for energy and climate as defined in point (11) of Article 2 of Regulation (EU) 2018/1999 of the European Parliament and of the Council (15) and a climate-neutral economy of the Union by 2050."

58 Regulation (EU) 2021/1229, Art. 1(2): "The Facility shall provide support benefitting Union territories facing serious social, environmental and economic challenges deriving from the transition process towards a climate-neutral economy of the Union by 2050."

59 Regulation (EU) 2021/1229, Art. 8.

3.2   Legal Bases and Financing via the Recovery Instrument

The financial instruments under the European Green Deal are based on provisions in Part Three (Union Policies and Internal Actions) Title XVII (Industry) and Title XVIII (Economic, Social and Territorial Cohesion) and Part Six (Institutional and Financial Provisions) Title II (Financial Provisions) of the TFEU. In all these cases, the proposals had to be adopted in the ordinary legislative procedure: the Recovery and Resilience Facility has been based on Articles 120 and 121 and Articles 174 and 175 TFEU and is thus a measure of the coordination of both economic policies and cohesion policy. REACT-EU has been based on Article 177 in conjunction with Article 322 lit a TFEU; it is thus a financial rule to "define the tasks, priority objectives and the organisation of the Structural Funds".[60] For InvestEU, the legal basis was Article 175(3) TFEU combined with Article 173 TFEU, under which the Union shall contribute to the objective of "ensuring the conditions necessary for the competitiveness of the Union's industry".[61] The Just Transition Fund and public sector loan facility have both been based on Articles 175 and 322(1)(a) TFEU), the former allowing for "specific actions prove necessary outside the Funds".[62] Thus, the majority of legal bases can be located in the Union's cohesion policy.

Most resources, however, stem from the Recovery Instrument in Council Regulation (EU) 2020/2094. The Recovery Instrument was based on Article 122 TFEU, and hence without the involvement of the European Parliament. Also, the Regulation does not specify the paragraph on which it was based. Since recitals (2), (5) and (6) refer to exceptional occurrences, it is likely, but surprisingly, to be Article 122(2) TFEU. That provision was used as a legal basis for the European Financial Stability Mechanism (EFSM),[63] but after that the Member States wanted to put the provision at rest (*Dornröschenschlaf*).[64] The Recovery Instrument provides EUR 750 billion (up to EUR 384.4 billion of non-repayable and repayable support, up to EUR 360 bn of loans and up to 5.6 billion of budgetary guarantees).[65] In comparison, the preceding MFF covered only EUR 371 billion of resources for economic, social and territorial cohesion.[66] Each of the financial instruments contains

---

60   Art. 177 TFEU.
61   Art. 173(1) and (3) TFEU.
62   Art. 175(3) TFEU.
63   Regulation (EU) 2010/407 of the Council of 11 May 2010 establishing a European financial stabilisation mechanism, OJ 2010 L 118/1.
64   *Smulders/Keppenne*, Art. 122 (ex-Artikel 100 EGV) [Gravierende Schwierigkeiten], in *Groeben/Schwarze/Hatje* (eds), Europäisches Unionsrecht[7] (2015) para 10.
65   Regulation (EU) 2020/2094, Art. 2.
66   Regulation (EU, Euratom) 2013/1311 of the Council of 2 December 2013 laying down the multiannual financial framework for the years 2014-2020, OJ 2013 L 347/884, Annex I.

a provision on the funds stemming from the Recovery Instrument (the remaining amount is dedicated to other minor instruments):[67]

- Up to EUR 312.5 billion is available as non-repayable funds and up to EUR 360 billion as loans by the Recovery and Resilience Facility.[68]
- Up to EUR 47.5 billion is to be spent as Structural Funds under REACT-EU.[69]
- The Just Transition Fund should comprise EUR 32.8 billion.[70]
- A guarantee of EUR 26.2 billion shall provide for the financing of EUR 372 billion under InvestEU.[71]
- The public sector loan facility shall be financed by EUR 250 billion of the Union budget and EUR 1,275 billion from assigned revenue.[72]

Hence, the resources of the main financing instrument of the European Green Deal have been adopted by the Council without the involvement of the European Parliament. Surprisingly, the Union's competences on environmental policy in the Articles 191 to 193 TFEU have not been used to adopt an instrument under the European Green Deal. Thus, a further analysis would have to scrutinise the appropriateness of the legal bases of these instruments in detail.

3.3   References to the General Regime of Rule of Law Conditionality

Several instruments of the European Green Deal (the Recovery and Resilience Facility,[73] REACT-EU,[74] the Just Transition Fund,[75] InvestEU[76] and the public sector loan facility[77]) contain links to the 'horizontal financial rules' of the newly established regime of conditionality in Regulation (EU, Euratom) 2020/2092. In this case, the reference can be found both in a recital and in the text of the Regulation: "The Facility shall be implemented by the Commission in direct management in accordance with the relevant rules adopted pursuant to Article 322 TFEU, in particular the Financial Regulation and the Regulation

---

67   *Council of the European Union*, Infographic – Next Generation EU – COVID-19 recovery package. Available at www.consilium.europa.eu/en/infographics/ngeu-covid-19-recovery-package/ (18 January 2021).
68   Regulation (EU) 2021/241, Art. 6.
69   Regulation (EU) 2020/2221, inserting Art. 92a to Regulation (EU) 1303/2013.
70   COM (2020) 460 final, Art. 3a.
71   Regulation (EU) 2021/523, Art. 4.
72   COM (2020) 453 final, Art. 4.
73   Regulation (EU) 2021/241, recital 71, Art. 8.
74   Regulation (EU) 2020/2221, recital 7.
75   Regulation (EU) 2021/1056, recital 9.
76   Regulation (EU) 2021/523, recital 65.
77   Regulation (EU) 2021/1229, recital 9.

(EU, Euratom) 2020/2092 of the European Parliament and of the Council."[78] In all other cases, the reference can merely be found in the recitals. First, the recitals state that the "[h]orizontal financial rules adopted by the European Parliament and the Council on the basis of Article 322 [TFEU] [...] apply to this Regulation".[79] Second, they specify these rules by mentioning the Financial Regulation (EU, Euratom) 2018/1046[80] and emphasising the general regime of conditionality for the protection of the Union budget, without explicitly referring to Regulation (EU, Euratom) 2020/2092.

The general regime of conditionality for the protection of the Union budget is the latest legislative outcome of countering a phenomenon called *rule of law and democratic backsliding*,[81] which refers to a deterioration of the respect for the common values of the EU listed in Article 2 TEU. Before that, the EU institutions addressed the crisis with the 2014 Rule of Law Framework[82] or procedures under Article 7 TEU[83] and Article 258 TFEU.[84] In 2018, the Commission adopted a proposal on the Protection of the Union Budget against Generalised Deficiencies as regards the Rule of Law.[85] In December 2020, the rule of law conditionality has been introduced to the EU's budgetary policy with Regulation (EC,

---

78   Regulation (EU) 2021/241, Art. 8.

79   Regulation (EU) 2020/2221, recital 7.

80   Regulation (EU, Euratom) 2018/1046 of the European Parliament and of the Council of 18 July 2018 on the financial rules applicable to the general budget of the Union, amending Regulations (EU) No 1296/2013, (EU) No 1301/2013, (EU) No 1303/2013, (EU) No 1304/2013, (EU) No 1309/2013, (EU) No 1316/2013, (EU) No 223/2014, (EU) No 283/2014, and Decision No 541/2014/EU and repealing Regulation (EU, Euratom) No 966/2012, OJ 2018 L 193/1.

81   On the term, *see Scheppele/Pech*, What is rule of law backsliding? Available at www.verfassungsblog.de/what-is-rule-of-law-backsliding/ (2 March 2018).

82   Communication from the Commission to the European Parliament and the Council, A new EU Framework to strengthen the Rule of Law, COM (2014) 158 final of 11 March 2014.

83   Resolution (EU) 2017/2131 of the European Parliament of 12 September 2018 on a proposal calling on the Council to determine, pursuant to Art. 7(1) of the Treaty on European Union, the existence of a clear risk of a serious breach by Hungary of the values on which the Union is founded, OJ 2019 C 433/66. Available at www.europarl.europa.eu/doceo/document/TA-8-2018-0340_EN.html.

84   Explicitly, ECJ C-192/18, *Commission v. Poland (Independence of Ordinary Courts)*, ECLI:EU:C:2019:924; ECJ C-619/18, *Commission v. Poland (Independence of the Supreme Court)*, ECLI:EU:C:2019:531; ECJ C-286/12, *Commission v. Hungary (Early retirement of judges)*, ECLI:EU:C:2012:687; ECJ C-66/18, *Commission v. Hungary (Higher Education)*, ECLI:EU:C:2020:792; ECJ C-78/18, *Commission v. Hungary (Transparency of associations)*, ECLI:EU:C:2020:476. More implicitly, ECJ C-64/16, *Associação Sindical dos Juízes Portugueses (ASJP)*, ECLI:EU:C:2018:117, paras 29-35; ECJ C-441/17, *Commission v. Poland (Forrest of Białowieska)*, ECLI:EU:C:2018:25.

85   Proposal for a Regulation of the European Parliament and of the Council on the protection of the Union's budget in case of generalised deficiencies as regards the rule of law in the Member States, COM (2018) 324 final of 2 May 2018. *See also, Staudinger*, Reflections on the general regime of conditionality for the protection of the union budget, in *Mayr/Orator* (eds), Populism, popular sovereignty and public reason Central and Eastern European Forum for Legal, Political, and Social Theory Yearbook (Peter Lang 2021); *Bogdandy/Łacny*, Suspension of EU funds for breaching the rule of law – a dose of tough love needed? Available at https://sieps.se/globalassets/publikationer/2020/2020_7epa.pdf? (June 2020); *Staudinger*, The conditionality mechanism as an instrument to protect the rule of law: COM (2018) 324 final, in *Kopetzki et al* (eds), Authoritäres vs Liberales Europa (2019) 183.

Euratom) 2020/2092.[86] As a result of lengthy discussions and threats to block the adoption of the MFF and the own resources decision, Regulation (EU, Euratom) 2020/2092 was adopted with the caveat that the enforcement will be delayed until after the Court of Justice's decision on a potential action for annulment and the Commission's adoption of guidelines on the application of the Regulation.[87] Voices in the literature have characterised the Conclusions of the European Council on the Commission's enforcement 'moratorium' illegal.[88] In March 2021, Hungary and Poland brought this action for annulment before the Court of Justice and sought to either annul the entire Regulation (EC, Euratom) 2020/2092 or Articles 4(1), 4(2)(h), 5(2) 5(3) penultimate sentence, 5(3) final sentence and 6(3) and (8) thereof.[89] In June 2021, the European Parliament indicated to bring an action for failure to act against the European Commission under Article 265 TFEU.[90] As of the beginning of September 2021, it remained to be seen whether Regulation (EU, Euratom) 2020/2092 will ever be enforced by the Commission.

4   CONCLUDING REMARKS

For the longest time, sustainable development and environmental protection have been stored on the shelf of EU objectives. As the title might suggest, with the European Green Deal, the Commission supposedly made an effort to infuse life into these objectives when it proposed several acts of secondary legislation and adopted numerous strategies to combat climate change. However, the European Green Deal is among many other things also 'green' though less dominantly than the title suggests. The instruments have been adopted on other competences (economic policy coordination, industry and cohesion policy) than those for environmental policy. Some 25 to 30% of funds will be dedicated to climate

---

86   Recently, the Regulation has been discussed in detail here: *Kirst*, Rule of law conditionality: The long-awaited step towards a solution of the rule of law crisis in the European Union? European Papers 2021/6, 101 (available at www.europeanpapers.eu/en/europeanforum/rule-law-conditionality-long-awaited-step-towards-solution-rule-law-crisis); *Łacny*, The rule of law conditionality under regulation no 2092/2020 – is it all about the money? Hague Journal on the Rule of Law 2021 (available at https://doi.org/10.1007/s40803-021-00154-6).

87   European Council meeting (10 and 11 December 2020) – Conclusions, EUCO 22/20. Available at www.consilium.europa.eu/media/47296/1011-12-20-euco-conclusions-en.pdf, para I.2.c.

88   On the illegality, *see Scheppele/Pech/Platon*, Compromising the rule of law while compromising on the rule of law. Available at https://verfassungsblog.de/compromising-the-rule-of-law-while-compromising-on-the-rule-of-law/ (13 December 2020).

89   Action brought on 11 March 2021 – *Hungary v. European Parliament and Council of the European Union* (Case C-156/21); Action brought on 11 March 2021 – Republic of Poland v European Parliament and Council of the European Union (Case C-157/21).

90   *Frankfurter Allgemeine Zeitung*, EU-Parlament will Kommission verklagen. Available at www.faz.net/aktuell/politik/ausland/wegen-polen-und-ungarn-eu-parlament-will-kommission-verklagen-17373601.html (4 June 2021).

objectives. The spending of the majority of funds – the Recovery and Resilience Facility and REACT-EU – must respect the 'do no harm' principle and pave the way for a green, digital and resilient recovery of the economy. Concurrently, the Commission adopted Regulation (EU, Euratom) 2020/2092 on a general regime of conditionality for the protection of the Union budget. In the event that a Member State does not respect the rule of law, payments of EU funds can be reduced or suspended. Consequently, access to economic recovery instruments has been made conditional to a) respect for the environment and b) respect for the rule of law when implementing the Union budget.

Whether these instruments, adopted mainly in the form of EU secondary legislation, will make a difference remains to be seen. While the effectiveness of the European Green Deal rather hinges on the question of monitoring compliance with the criteria and on technical aspects, namely whether it is not too little too late, the effectiveness of the EU's rule of law mechanism also depends on the Commission's zeal to use its new powers.

BIBLIOGRAPHY

Bogdandy/Łacny, Suspension of EU funds for breaching the rule of law – a dose of tough love needed? Available at https://sieps.se/globalassets/publikationer/2020/2020_7epa.pdf? (June 2020).

Der Spiegel, Air France soll Inlandsflüge zugunsten von Schnellzügen streichen. Available at www.spiegel.de/auto/air-france-soll-inlandsfluege-zugunsten-von-schnellzuegen-streichen-a-a1dabbeb-9e61-43ab-b707-09378a5a3616 (5 May 2020).

Die Zeit, Annalena Baerbock will Kurzstreckenflüge auf Dauer abschaffen. Available at www.zeit.de/politik/deutschland/2021-05/gruene-annalena-baerbock-kurzstreckenfluege-solar-kimaschutz (16 May 2021).

European Commission, EU climate action and the European Green Deal. Available at https://ec.europa.eu/clima/policies/eu-climate-action_en (6 June 2021).

European Commission, The Just Transition Mechanism: making sure no one is left behind. Available at https://ec.europa.eu/info/strategy/priorities-2019-2024/european-green-deal/actions-being-taken-eu/just-transition-mechanism_en (6 June 2021).

European Investment Bank, EU Bank launches ambitious new climate strategy and Energy Lending Policy. Available at www.eib.org/en/press/all/2019-313-eu-bank-launches-ambitious-new-climate-strategy-and-energy-lending-policy (14 November 2019).

Frankfurter Allgemeine Zeitung, EU-Parlament will Kommission verklagen. Available at www.faz.net/aktuell/politik/ausland/wegen-polen-und-ungarn-eu-parlament-will-kommission-verklagen-17373601.html (4 June 2021).

Frankfurter Allgemeine Zeitung, Lufthansa will Auflagen der EU-Kommission annehmen. Available at www.faz.net/aktuell/wirtschaft/unternehmen/regierung-und-eu-kommission-einigen-sich-bei-lufthansa-rettung-16793046.html (30 May 2020).

Huck, Die EU und die Globale Agenda 2030 der Vereinten Nationen: Reflexion, Strategie und rechtliche Umsetzung, EuZW 2019/30, 581.

Kirst, Rule of law conditionality: The long-awaited step towards a solution of the rule of law crisis in the European Union? European Papers 2021/6, 101. Available at www.europeanpapers.eu/en/europeanforum/rule-law-conditionality-long-awaited-step-towards-solution-rule-law-crisis.

Krämer, Artikel 11 [Umweltschutz; Querschnittsklausel], in *Groeben/Schwarze/Hatje* (eds), Europäisches Unionsrecht[7] (2015).

Łacny, The rule of law conditionality under regulation no 2092/2020 – is it all about the money? Hague Journal on the Rule of Law 2021, 79. Available at https://doi.org/10.1007/s40803-021-00154-6.

Le Quéré/Jackson/Jones et al, Temporary reduction in daily global CO2 emissions during the COVID-19 forced confinement, Nature Climate Change 2020, 647. Available at www.nature.com/articles/s41558-020-0797-x (19 May 2020).

Scheppele/Pech, What is rule of law backsliding? Available at www.verfassungsblog.de/what-is-rule-of-law-backsliding/ (2 March 2018).

Scheppele/Pech/Platon, Compromising the rule of law while compromising on the rule of law. Available at https://verfassungsblog.de/compromising-the-rule-of-law-while-compromising-on-the-rule-of-law/ (13 December 2020).

Smulders/Keppenne, Art. 122 (ex-Artikel 100 EGV) [Gravierende Schwierigkeiten], in *Gro-eben/Schwarze/Hatje* (eds), Europäisches Unionsrecht[7] (2015).

Staudinger, Reflections on the general regime of conditionality for the protection of the union budget, in *Mayr/Orator* (eds), Populism, popular sovereignty and public reason Central and Eastern European Forum for Legal, Political, and Social Theory Yearbook (forthcoming, Peter Lang 2021).

Staudinger, The conditionality mechanism as an instrument to protect the rule of law: COM (2018) 324 final, in *Kopetzki et al* (eds), Authoritäres vs Liberales Europe (2019).

Süddeutsche Zeitung, Bund stellt Umweltauflagen für Lufthansa-Rettungspaket. Available at www.sueddeutsche.de/wirtschaft/luftverkehr-frankfurt-am-main-bund-stellt-umwelt auflagen-fuer-lufthansa-rettungspaket-dpa.urn-newsml-dpa-com-20090101-200525-99-182542 (25 May 2020).

United Nations Department of Economic and Social Affairs, Sustainable Development Goals. Available at https://sdgs.un.org (6 June 2020).

Cases

ECJ C-156/21, Action brought on 11 March 2021 – *Hungary v. European Parliament and Council of the European Union* [case in progress].

ECJ C-64/16, *Associação Sindical dos Juízes Portugueses (ASJP)*, ECLI:EU:C:2018:117.

ECJ C-286/12, *Commission v. Hungary (Early retirement of judges)*, ECLI:EU:C:2012:687.

ECJ C-66/18, *Commission v. Hungary (Higher Education)*, ECLI:EU:C:2020:792.

ECJ C-78/18, *Commission v. Hungary (Transparency of associations)*, ECLI:EU:C:2020:476.

ECJ C-441/17, *Commission v. Poland (Forrest of Białowieska)*, ECLI:EU:C:2018:25.

ECJ C-192/18, *Commission v. Poland (Independence of Ordinary Courts)*, ECLI:EU:C:2019:924.

ECJ C-619/18, *Commission v. Poland (Independence of the Supreme Court)*, ECLI:EU:C:2019:531.

EU Documents and Legislative Acts

Amended proposal for a Council Regulation laying down the multiannual financial framework for the years 2021 to 2027, COM (2020) 443 final of 28 May 2020.

Communication from the Commission to the European Parliament, the European Council, the Council, the European Economic and Social Committee, the Committee of the Regions and the European Investment Bank, A Clean Planet for all. A European strategic long-term vision for a prosperous, modern, competitive and cli-mate neutral economy, COM (2018) 773 final, 28 November 2018.

Communication from the Commission to the European Parliament, the European Council, the Council, the European Economic and Social Committee and the Committee of the Regions, A Modern Budget for a Union that Protects, Empowers and Defends the Multiannual Financial Framework for 2021-2027, COM (2018) 321 final of 2 May 2018.

Communication from the Commission to the European Parliament, the Council, the European Economic and Social Committee and the Committee of the Regions, A new Circular Economy Action Plan For a cleaner and more competitive Europe, COM (2020) 98 final of 11 March 2020.

Communication from the Commission to the European Parliament and the Council, A new EU Framework to strengthen the Rule of Law, COM (2014) 158 final of 11 March 2014.

Communication from the Commission to the European Parliament, the Council, the European Economic and Social Committee and the Committee of the Regions, European Climate Pact, COM (2020) 788 final of 9 December 2020.

Communication from the Commission to the European Parliament, the Council, the European Economic and Social Committee and the Committee of the Regions, Forging a climate-resilient Europe – the new EU Strategy on Adaptation to Climate Change, COM (2021) 82 final of 24 February 2021.

Communication from the Commission to the European Parliament, the Council, the European Council, the European Economic and Social Committee and the Committee of the Regions, Stepping up Europe's 2030 climate ambition. Investing in a climate-neutral future for the benefit of our people, COM (2020) 562 final of 17 September 2020.

Communication from the Commission to the European Parliament, the Council, the European Economic and Social Committee and the Committee of the Regions, Sustainable Europe Investment Plan European Green Deal Investment Plan, COM (2020) 21 final of 14 January 2020.

Communication from the Commission, The European Green Deal, COM (2019) 640 final of 11 December 2019.

Decision (EU) 2020/2228 of the European Parliament and of the Council of 23 December 2020 on a European Year of Rail (2021), OJ 2020 L 437/108.

European Council meeting (10 and 11 December 2020) – Conclusions, EUCO 22/20. Available at www.consilium.europa.eu/media/47296/1011-12-20-euco-conclusions-en.pdf.

Proposal for a Council Regulation laying down the multiannual financial framework for the years 2021 to 2027, COM (2018) 322 final of 2 May 2018.

Proposal for a Regulation of the European Parliament and of the Council establishing the framework for achieving climate neutrality and amending Regulation (EU) 2018/1999 (European Climate Law), COM (2020) 80 final of 4 March 2020.

Proposal for a Regulation of the European Parliament and of the Council on the protection of the Union's budget in case of generalised deficiencies as regards the rule of law in the Member States, COM (2018) 324 final of 2 May 2018.

Regulation (EU) 2010/407 of the Council of 11 May 2010 establishing a European financial stabilisation mechanism, OJ 2010 L 118/1.

Regulation (EU, Euratom) 2013/1311 of the Council of 2 December 2013 laying down the multiannual financial framework for the years 2014-2020, OJ 2013 L 347/884.

Regulation (EU) 2020/2094 of the Council of 14 December 2020 establishing a European Union Recovery Instrument to support the recovery in the aftermath of the COVID-19 crisis, OJ 2020 L 433I/23.

Regulation (EU) 1293/2013 of the European Parliament and of the Council of 11 December 2013 on the establishment of a Programme for the Environment and Climate Action (LIFE) and repealing Regulation (EC) 614/2007, OJ 2013 L347/185.

Regulation (EU) 1303/2013 of the European Parliament and of the Council of 17 December 2013 laying down common provisions on the European Regional Development Fund, the European Social Fund, the Cohesion Fund, the European Agricultural Fund for Rural Development and the European Maritime and Fisheries Fund and laying down general provisions on the European Regional Development Fund, the European Social Fund, the Cohesion Fund and the European Maritime and Fisheries Fund and repealing Council Regulation (EC) 1083/2006, OJ 2013 L 347/320.

Regulation (EU, Euratom) 2018/1046 of the European Parliament and of the Council of 18 July 2018 on the financial rules applicable to the general budget of the Union, amending Regulations (EU) No 1296/2013, (EU) No 1301/2013, (EU) No 1303/2013, (EU) No 1304/2013, (EU) No 1309/2013, (EU) No 1316/2013, (EU) No 223/2014, (EU) No 283/2014, and Decision No 541/2014/EU and repealing Regulation (EU, Euratom) No 966/2012, OJ 2018 L 193/1.

Regulation (EU) 2018/1999 of the European Parliament and of the Council of 11 December 2018 on the Governance of the Energy Union and Climate Action, amending Regulations (EC) 663/2009 and (EC) 715/2009 of the European Parliament and of the Council, Directives 94/22/EC, 98/70/EC, 2009/31/EC, 2009/73/EC, 2010/31/EU, 2012/27/EU and 2013/30/EU of the European Parliament and of the Council, Council Directives 2009/119/EC and (EU) 2015/652 and repealing Regulation (EU) 525/2013 of the European Parliament and of the Council, OJ 2018 L 328/1.

Regulation (EU) 2020/852 of the European Parliament and of the Council of 18 June 2020 on the establishment of a framework to facilitate sustainable investment, and amending Regulation (EU) 2019/2088, OJ 2020 L 198/13.

Regulation (EU, Euratom) 2020/2092 of the European Parliament and of the Council of 16 December 2020 on a general regime of conditionality for the protection of the Union budget, OJ 2020 L 433I/1.

Regulation (EU) 2020/2221 of the European Parliament and of the Council of 23 December 2020 amending Regulation (EU) 1303/2013 as regards additional resources and implementing arrangements to provide assistance for fostering crisis repair in the context of the COVID-19 pandemic and its social consequences and for preparing a green, digital and resilient recovery of the economy (REACT-EU), OJ 2020 L 437/30.

Regulation (EU) 2021/241 of the European Parliament and of the Council of 12 February 2021 establishing the Recovery and Resilience Facility, OJ 2021 L 57/17.

Regulation (EU) 2021/523 of the European Parliament and of the Council of 24 March 2021 establishing the InvestEU Programme and amending Regulation (EU) 2015/1017, OJ 2021 L 107/30.

Regulation (EU) 2021/1056 of the European Parliament and of the Council of 24 June 2021 establishing the Just Transition Fund [2021] OJ L 231/1.

Regulation (EU) 2021/1119 of the European Parliament and of the Council of 30 June 2021 establishing the framework for achieving climate neutrality and amending Regulations (EC) No 401/2009 and (EU) 2018/1999 ('European Climate Law') [2021] OJ L 243/1.

Resolution (EU) 2017/2131 of the European Parliament of 12 September 2018 on a proposal calling on the Council to determine, pursuant to Article 7(1) of the Treaty on European Union, the existence of a clear risk of a serious breach by Hungary of the values on which the Union is founded, OJ 2019 C 433/66. Available at www.europarl.europa.eu/doceo/document/TA-8-2018-0340_EN.html.

OTHER DOCUMENTS

Conference of the Parties, Adoption of the Paris Agreement (adopted on 12 December 2015) UN Doc FCCC/CP/2015/L.9/Rev/1.

Kyoto Protocol to the United Nations Framework Convention on Climate Change (adopted 11 December 1997, entered into force 16 February 2005) 2303 UNTS 148.

United Nations Framework Convention on Climate Change (adopted 9 May 1992, entered into force 21 March 1994) 1771 UNTS 107.

United Nations General Assembly, Transforming our world: the 2030 Agenda for Sustainable Development (adopted on 25 September 2015) A/RES/71/1.

THE ECUADORIAN CHEVRON JUDGMENT

Blueprint for a Neoconstitutional Environmental Law?

Andreas Gutmann

1   BACKGROUND

The damages caused by the oil extraction in the Ecuadorian Amazon by Texaco and its successors since the 1960s are one of the most devastating ecological disasters the planet has ever seen. Millions of gallons of crude oil and wastes were spilled.[1] For decades, the Chevron saga has kept courts busy all around the globe.[2] Recently, the Ecuadorian constitutional court made its contribution to this never-ending story by rejecting a constitutional complaint filed by Chevron Corporation in which the company tried to turn down the obligation to pay billions of dollars to the aggrieved parties (*afectados*) in the environmental disaster. Several Ecuadorian courts had considered the company liable for causing severe harm to both the environment and the indigenous and campesino population, a finding that was upheld by the Supreme Court in 2013.[3] Shortly after the constitutional judgment was issued, the Permanent Court of Arbitration at The Hague condemned the Ecuadorian state to refrain from enforcing the judgments.[4] I will focus on the Ecuadorian constitutional ruling, which is groundbreaking for environmental constitutional law and human rights. Furthermore, it demonstrates the normative force of the neoconstitutional model of the Ecuadorian constitution, which – far from merely being a 'wish list'[5] or a kind of 'constitutional poetry' ("Verfassungslyrik")[6] – forcefully aims at strengthening human and environmental rights.

---

1   *Miller*, Ecuador: Texaco Leaves Trail of Destruction, https://corpwatch.org/article/ecuador-texaco-leaves-trail-destruction (30 November 2003).

2   For the background *see Franzki/Horst*, On the Critical Potential of Law – And Its Limits – Double Fragmentation of Law in Chevron Corp. v. Ecuador, in: *Blome/Fischer-Lescano* (eds), Contested Regime Collisions – Norm Fragmentation in World Society (2016) 347; *Joseph*, Protracted Lawfare: The Tale of Chevron Texaco in the Amazon, JHRE 2012/3, 70.

3   Corte Nacional de Justicia 12 September 2013, Sentencia N.° 174-2012.

4   *See Sturm*, Ecuador: Internationaler Gerichtshof annulliert Urteil gegen Erdölkonzern Chevron, https://amerika21.de/2018/09/212708/ecuador-chevron-haag-urteil (16 September 2018).

5   *Nolte*, Verfassungspopulismus und Verfassungswandel in Lateinamerika, GIGA Focus Lateinamerika 2009/2, 5.

6   *Kischel*, Rechtsvergleichung (2015) 664.

First, it seems appropriate to sum up the Ecuadorian constitutional background. In 2008, shortly after President Rafael Correa took office, a new constitution was enacted.[7] This constitution (Constitución de la República del Ecuador, CRE[8]) can be seen as a prime example of the so-called Latin American Neoconstitutionalism,[9] a school that has steadily gained importance since the nineties.[10] Constitutions are considered as initiating power for a wide range of social (and, at least in the Ecuadorian case, also ecological) transformations of the state.[11] Neoconstitutional constitutions grant numerous social, collective, indigenous, and ecological rights that are put on an equal footing with traditional liberal human rights.[12] The CRE is even one step ahead for being the first constitution that recognizes nature as a bearer of rights.[13] Additionally, it provides legal actions in favour of the environment (Art. 88, 71, 397 No. 1 CRE)[14] as well as very strict environmental liability rules (Art. 396 CRE et seq.).

Scholars and activists have pointed out that courts often fail in implementing this paradigm shift[15] and rather bolster the neoextractivist dogma[16] of the government. At least for the present case, this critique misses the point. The judgment of the constitutional court clearly seeks the optimization of ecological and collective rights.

2   The Judgment

The court had to decide a so-called acción extraordinaria de protección lawsuit,[17] i.e., a constitutional remedy filed by Chevron in order to declare void the rulings that condemned

---

7   *Becker*, Correa, Indigenous Movements, and the Writing of a New Constitution in Ecuador, Latin American Perspectives 2011/38, 47; *Salgado Pesantes*, El proceso constituyente del Ecuador – Algunas reflexiones, Revista Instituto Interamericano de Derechos Humanos 2008/47, 205.

8   An English translation is available at https://pdba.georgetown.edu/Constitutions/Ecuador/english08.html (31 January 2011).

9   *Melo*, Derechos de la Naturaleza, globalización y cambio climático, Línea Sur 2013/5, 43.

10   *Viciano Pastor/Martínez Dalmau*, Aspectos generales del nuevo constitucionalismo latinoamericano, in: *Avila Linzán*, (eds), Política, justicia y constitución, (2011) 167.

11   *Narváez Quiñónez/Narváez*, Derecho ambiental en clave neoconstitucional – Enfoque político (2012) 136.

12   *Storini*, Las Garantiás Constitucionales de los Derechos Fundamentales en la Constitución Ecuatoriana de 2008, in: *Andrade Ubidia/Grijalva/Storini* (eds), La Nueva Constitución del Ecuador – Estado, derechos e instituciones (2009) 287.

13   *Gutmann*, Pachamama As a Legal Person? Rights of Nature and Indigenous Thinking in Ecuador, in: *Corrigan/Oksanen* (eds), Rights of Nature: A Re-examination (2021) 36.

14   *Cf.* at length *Guarando Mendoza*, Acciones jurídicas para establecer responsabilidades por daño ambiental en el Ecuador (2010).

15   *E.g. Guarando Mendoza*, Acciones jurídicas para establecer responsabilidades por daño ambiental en el Ecuador (2010) 129.

16   *See Gutmann/Valle Franco*, Extraktivismus und das Gute Leben – Buen Vivir/Vivir Bien und der Umgang des Rechts mit nichterneuerbaren Ressourcen in Ecuador und Bolivien, Kritische Justiz 2019/52, 58.

17   For the background of this constitutional remedy *see Tschentscher/Lehner*, The Latin American Model of Constitutional Jurisdiction: Amparo and Judicial Review, SSRN Journal 2013; *Brewer-Carías*, The Amparo

the company to pay reparations to the people affected by the environmental disaster. Thus, Chevron sued the Ecuadorian state, and the *afectados* did not directly take part in the proceedings. Since the Ecuadorian constitutional court does not have the power to fully review the findings of the lower courts, it limited itself to an assessment of the constitutional rights that Chevron considered had been violated.[18] In accordance with that, the court did not substantially review the alleged procedural fraud that Chevron accuses the victims of. Some of the core arguments provided by the court are set forth in what follows.

2.1 Human Rights and Ecological Damages

The court thoroughly discussed the agreement that releases Chevron from liability vis-à-vis the Ecuadorian state, signed by Ecuador and Chevron (respectively, its predecessor TexPet) in 1995.[19] The agreement explicitly excludes private claims for indemnity brought forward by third parties, without, however, specifying whether this provision should also apply to diffuse or collective claims such as those of the *afectados*. This did not trouble the court. In fact, the CRE does not differentiate between individual and collective rights.[20] The court, therefore, explained that the agreement could only bind the parties, which are Chevron and the Ecuadorian state.[21] The state could not dispose of its citizens' fundamental rights. The court somehow constitutionalized the victim's claim by tracing it back to the fundamental right to an intact environment.[22] Chevron, a private company, is bound by these fundamental rights that are concretized by environmental liability law. The state has no authority to derogate from this commitment.[23]

2.2 Strict Liability

Furthermore, Chevron alleged that the lower courts applied the 1999 Environmental Management Law (Ley de Gestión Ambiental, LGA) and the principle of strict liability in environmental liability cases retroactively.[24] The company's extractive activities at the Amazon had already ceased when this law was adopted. However, Article 43 LGA increases

as an Instrument of a Ius Constitutionale Commune, in: *von Bogdandy/Ferrer Mac-Gregor* (eds), Transformative Constitutionalism in Latin America – The Emergence of a New Ius Commune (2017) 171.

18 Corte Constitucional 27 July 2018, Sentencia N.° 230-18-SEP-CC, 55 ff.

19 *Id.*, 86 ff.

20 *Gutmann*, Pachamama as a Legal Person? Rights of Nature and Indigenous Thinking in Ecuador, in: *Corrigan/Oksanen* (eds), Rights of Nature: A Re-examination (2021) 43.

21 Corte Constitucional 27 July 2018, Sentencia N.° 230-18-SEP-CC, 94 ff.

22 *Cf. id.*, 91 ff.

23 Corte Constitucional 27 July 2018, Sentencia N.° 230-18-SEP-CC, 98.

24 *Id.*, 99 ff.

indemnity in environmental liability cases by 10% over the real amount of damage and therefore enables victims to claim a kind of punitive damage. Additionally, the courts applied strict liability, which is now also provided by Article 396 CRE in environmental liability cases. Hence, it was not relevant whether Chevron acted negligently, which used to be a severely disputed topic in previous lawsuits. The constitutional court had to decide whether these newly established principles could be applied to the present case. It tried to balance Chevron's legitimate interest in legal security and the *afectado*'s right to compensation.[25] The latter gained further weight through the *in dubio pro natura* principle, which plays an important role within the 2008 constitution.[26] This principle states that in case of doubt, legal rules must be interpreted as favourably for the environment as possible. The court, in applying the *in dubio pro natura*, held that the environmental rights granted by the constitution overrule legal security and allow the retroactive application of legal rules in this specific case.[27]

Apparently frightened by its own statement, the court tries to downplay the retroactive character of the LGA and the application of the strict liability doctrine in the following passages. Strict liability in case of hazardous activities was well known by the Ecuadorian civil code when Chevron started exploitation.[28] According to the court, the CRE itself does not establish strict liability but only concretizes an already existing concept.[29]

2.3   Continuing Injustice

The court also used the so-called continuing injustice argument, which might revolutionize environmental liability law.[30] The judges held that damages occurred from the beginning of Chevron's harmful conduct till the date of the judgment and might even aggravate over the years.[31] The nonreparation, therefore, continuously harms the *afectados* and the environment. We thus do not need to apply current laws retroactively for the infringements that are currently occurring. The dubio pro natura principle requires application of the law, which mostly favours environmental protection, which in the present case were the LGA and CRE. The possible consequences of applying the continuing injustice argument to environmental liability law can hardly be overestimated. Strictly speaking, courts in most cases have to apply the existing laws, at least if the legislature takes the nonregression principle in environmental law seriously.

---

25   *Id.*, 106 ff.
26   *Id.*, 107 ff.
27   *Id.*, 112.
28   *Id.*, 114 ff.
29   *Id.*, 115.
30   *Id.*, 110 ff.
31   *Id.*, 111.

2.4   Acquired Rights to Pollute?

Chevron also argued that the lower court's judgments impaired its legitimate expectations in the 1995 agreement and the legal norms prevailing at the time of oil exploitation at the Amazon. The company's legitimate expectations were supposed to form so-called 'acquired rights' (*derechos adquiridos*), creating a legal position that is protected against privation by the constitution. The court apodictically rejected this line of argument. It reasoned that the so-called acquired rights cannot restrict the constitutional right to the environment. The court's reasoning was based on the effective realization of the right to environment and the nonprescription of environmental liability (Art. 396 CRE)[32]. In a nutshell, it concluded that "[...] nobody holds an acquired right to pollute the environment [...]".[33] If we take this literally, the consequences will be tremendous. Strictly speaking, mining concessions and the permission of industrial plants consist merely of granting such rights.

3   CONCLUSION

Whether the constitutional judgment opens a new chapter in environmental jurisprudence remains to be seen. If its line of reasoning is taken seriously, it definitely will. The court undertakes promising efforts to overcome the shortcomings of environmental liability law by strictly stressing its interdependencies with human rights. It thereby underlines the CRE's attempt to establish a new understanding of human-nature relationships that is based on relationality and respect and tries to overcome the supposed dichotomy between nature and culture.[34] Its neoconstitutional impetus is obvious since it is driven by the will to expand human and environmental rights as far as possible.

It also remains to be seen whether the judgment will conclude the Chevron saga. The CRE's attitude toward international arbitration is quite clear. Article 422 para 1 reads:

> Treaties or international instruments where the Ecuadorian State yields its sovereign jurisdiction to international arbitration entities in disputes involving contracts or trade between the State and natural persons or legal entities cannot be entered into.

---

32   *Id.*, 112.
33   *Id.*
34   *Gutmann*, Pachamama as a Legal Person? Rights of Nature and Indigenous Thinking in Ecuador, in: *Corrigan/Oksanen* (eds), Rights of Nature: A Re-examination (2021).

From an Ecuadorian perspective, the last word has been spoken since the constitutional court authoritatively interpreted the constitution. Whether international arbitration law can meet with this green constitutionalism is still doubtful.

BIBLIOGRAPHY

Ávila Santamaría, El neoconstitucionalismo transformador – El estado y el derecho en la Constitución de 2008 (2011).

Becker, Correa, Indigenous Movements, and the Writing of a New Constitution in Ecuador, Latin American Perspectives 2011/38, 47.

Brewer-Carías, The Amparo as an Instrument of a Ius Constitutionale Commune, in *Bogdandy/Ferrer Mac-Gregor et al.* (eds.), Transformative Constitutionalism in Latin America – The Emergence of a New Ius Commune (2017).

Franzki/Horst, On the Critical Potential of Law – And Its Limits – Double Fragmentation of Law in Chevron Corp. v. Ecuador, in *Blome/Fischer-Lescano et al.* (eds.), Contested Regime Collisions – Norm Fragmentation in World Society (2016).

Guarando Mendoza, Acciones jurídicas para establecer responsabilidades por daño ambiental en el Ecuador (2010).

Gutmann, Pachamama as a Legal Person? Rights of Nature and Indigenous Thinking in Ecuador, in *Corrigan/Oksanen* (eds.), Rights of Nature: A Re-examination (2021).

Gutmann/Valle Franco, Extraktivismus und das Gute Leben – Buen Vivir/Vivir Bien und der Umgang des Rechts mit nichterneuerbaren Ressourcen in Ecuador und Bolivien, Kritische Justiz 2019/52, 58.

Joseph, Protracted Lawfare: The Tale of Chevron Texaco in the Amazon, JHRE 2012/3, 70.

Kischel, Rechtsvergleichung (2015).

Melo, Derechos de la Naturaleza, globalización y cambio climático, Línea Sur 2013/5, 43.

Miller, Ecuador: Texaco Leaves Trail of Destruction, https://corpwatch.org/article/ecuador-texaco-leaves-trail-destruction (30 November 2003).

Narváez Quiñónez/Narváez, Derecho ambiental en clave neoconstitucional – Enfoque político (2012).

Noguera Fernández, El neoconstitucionalismo andino – ¿una superación de la contradicción entre democracia y justicia constitucional? R.V.A.P. 2011, 167.

Nolte, Verfassungspopulismus und Verfassungswandel in Lateinamerika, GIGA Focus Lateinamerika (2009).

Salgado Pesantes, El proceso constituyente del Ecuador – Algunas reflexiones, Revista Instituto Interamericano de Derechos Humanos 2008/47, 205.

Storini, Las Garantiás Constitucionales de los Derechos Fundamentales en la Constitución Ecuatoriana de 2008, in *Andrade Ubidia/Grijalva/Storini* (eds.), La Nueva Constitución del Ecuador – Estado, derechos e instituciones (2009).

Sturm, Ecuador: Internationaler Gerichtshof annulliert Urteil gegen Erdölkonzern Chevron, https://amerika21.de/2018/09/212708/ecuador-chevron-haag-urteil (16 September 2018).

Tschentscher/Lehner, The Latin American Model of Constitutional Jurisdiction: Amparo and Judicial Review, SSRN Journal 2013.

Viciano Pastor/Martínez Dalmau, Aspectos generales del nuevo constitucionalismo latinoamericano, in *Avila Linzán* (eds.), Política, justicia y constitución (2011).

CASES

Corte Constitucional 27 July 2018, Sentencia N.° 230-18-SEP-CC.

Corte Nacional de Justicia 12 September 2013, N.° 174-2012.

List of editors and authors

Carlotta Garofalo

Carlotta Garofalo is a Doctoral Researcher at the Institute of Public Law and Political Sciences and a member of the Doctoral Program Climate Change at the University of Graz (Austria).

Andreas Gutmann

Andreas Gutmann is legal trainee (Rechtsreferendar) at the Kammergericht Berlin and Research Assistant at the Centre of European Law and Politics (ZERP), University of Bremen (Germany).

Miriam Hofer

Miriam Hofer is a Post-Doctoral Researcher at the Institute of Public Law and Political Science at the University of Graz (Austria).

Ferdinand Kerschner

Ferdinand Kerschner is a retired Professor of Civil and Environmental Law of the Johannes Kepler University Linz (Austria) and Vice President of the Forum Science and Environment. He is further a Visiting Professor at the Charles University Prague (Czech Republic).

Lydia Omuko-Jung

Lydia Omuko-Jung is a Kenyan Attorney and currently a Doctoral Researcher at the Institute of Public Law and Political Science and in the Doctoral Program Climate Change at the University of Graz. She is also a Legal Analyst at the Climate Change Litigation Initiative (C2LI) at the University of Strathclye, Glasgow (Scotland).

Christoph Romirer

Christoph Romirer is a Doctoral Researcher at the Institute of Public Law and Political Science at the University of Graz (Austria).

Oliver C. Ruppel

Oliver C. Ruppel is Professor of Public and International Law at the Faculty of Law at Stellenbosch University (South Africa) and the Director of its Development and Rule of Law Programme (DROP). He is further the Co-Director of the Research Center for Climate Law ClimLaw: Graz (Austria); distinguished Fellow at the Fraunhofer Centre for

International Management and Knowledge Economy, Leipzig (Germany); and Professor Extraordinaire at various Universities around the world.

Markus Scharler
Markus Scharler is a former research associate at the Institute for Public Law and Political Science at the University of Graz. He now works as a jurist in the federal state of Styria (Austria).

Eva Schulev-Steindl
Eva Schulev-Steindl is Professor of Public and Commercial Law and Vice-Dean at the Faculty of Law at the University of Graz (Austria). She is the Founding Director of the Research Center for Climate Law ClimLaw: Graz.

Jaap Spier
Jaap Spier is former Advocate-General of the Supreme Court of the Netherlands: Senior Associate at the Institute for Sustainability Leadership at the University of Cambridge (UK). He is Honorary Professor of Global Challenges at Stellenbosch University (South Africa) and Senior Fellow at the Global Justice Programme Yale (USA).

Isabel Staudinger
Isabel Staudinger is a postdoctoral researcher at the Department of Public Law, Public International and European Law at the University of Salzburg (Austria) and in the European Constitutional Court Network (www.eccn.at) research project.

www.ingramcontent.com/pod-product-compliance
Lightning Source LLC
Chambersburg PA
CBHW080555220326
41599CB00032B/6488